SOVEIIREIGN

A CELEBRATION OF FORTY YEARS OF SERVICE

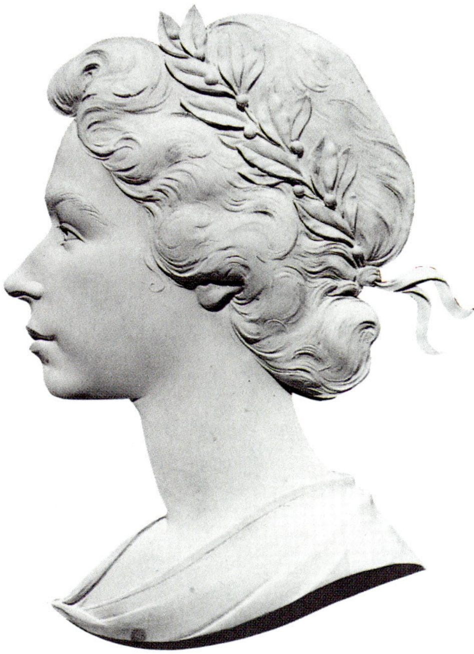

INTRODUCED BY

JOHN JULIUS NORWICH

HER MAJESTY THE QUEEN'S 40TH ANNIVERSARY

C&B
COLLINS & BROWN

SOVEREIGN

HER MAJESTY THE QUEEN'S
40TH ANNIVERSARY

The SOVEREIGN Exhibition is commissioned by The Royal Anniversary Trust as part of the programme of celebration of the 40th anniversary of the Queen's accession to the throne.

SOVEREIGN was designed by the Royal College of Art, presented at the Victoria and Albert Museum and sponsored by The Daily Telegraph, Pearson and Reed International.

The Daily Telegraph · PEARSON · REED INTERNATIONAL

INTRODUCTION

When the Royal Anniversary Trust decided to commission the SOVEREIGN exhibition, they knew that they would be breaking entirely new ground. No previous exhibition in the history of these islands has attempted to explain the nature of our British monarchy; nor has one ever been focused on a single reigning monarch. And this, it must be admitted, is hardly surprising: in earlier days any such exhibition would probably been seen a *Lèse-majesté*, and would anyway have been virtually impossible without modern technology.

But, as SOVEREIGN will make abundantly clear, much else has also occurred in the four decades that have so far marked the reign of Queen Elizabeth II. Not only has our exhibition technology advanced by leaps and bounds; there have also been changes, almost as dramatic, in our conception of the monarchy itself. Although it remains as popular as ever it was, the vastly increased powers of the press, radio and, above all, television have brought it far closer to us all than ever before. In Victorian days the Queen was so remote from those over whom she ruled that it caused relatively little controversy when, in the sorrow of her young widowhood, she withdrew almost completely from view for a quarter of a century, performing hardly any ceremonial duties and scarcely ever appearing in public. For Elizabeth II, such conduct would be unthinkable. But then Victoria, travelling incognito, could pass unrecognized among the vast majority of her subjects: the face of the present Queen, seen daily not only in stylized form on coins, banknotes and postage stamps but also in its more familar image on the newspaper page and the television screen, is better known, perhaps, than any other on earth. For most people of the nineteenth century, Victoria was Queen and Empress and that was that. For us, her great-great-granddaughter possesses a whole extra dimension. She is royal, certainly; but she is also a wife, a mother and a grandmother six times over. In many ways her life is astonishingly different from ours; in others, it is very much the same.

This unique combination of differences and similarities lies at the root of the perennial fascination which most of us feel, whether we admit it or not, about the Queen and her family – a fascination which affects not just those who actually recognize her as their ruler but extends to millions of others across the world, a tiny but none the less remarkable proportion of whom have actually seen and even met her – for few people on earth have travelled more widely than she has, or shaken more hands. Fascination, inevitably, breeds curiosity – a very natural desire to know more about this essentially ordinary family which finds itself placed, purely by reason of heredity and through no fault of its own, in a most extraordinary position. And it is partly to satisfy this curiosity that the SOVEREIGN exhibition has been conceived.

Partly, but by no means entirely: for SOVEREIGN is above all a celebration, intended to give proper recognition to the Queen's forty years on the throne. In the history of our monarchy, such a span is rare indeed. Of her thirty-nine predecessors since the Norman Conquest, only five – Henry III, Edward III, Elizabeth I, George III and Victoria – managed to equal such a figure, and,

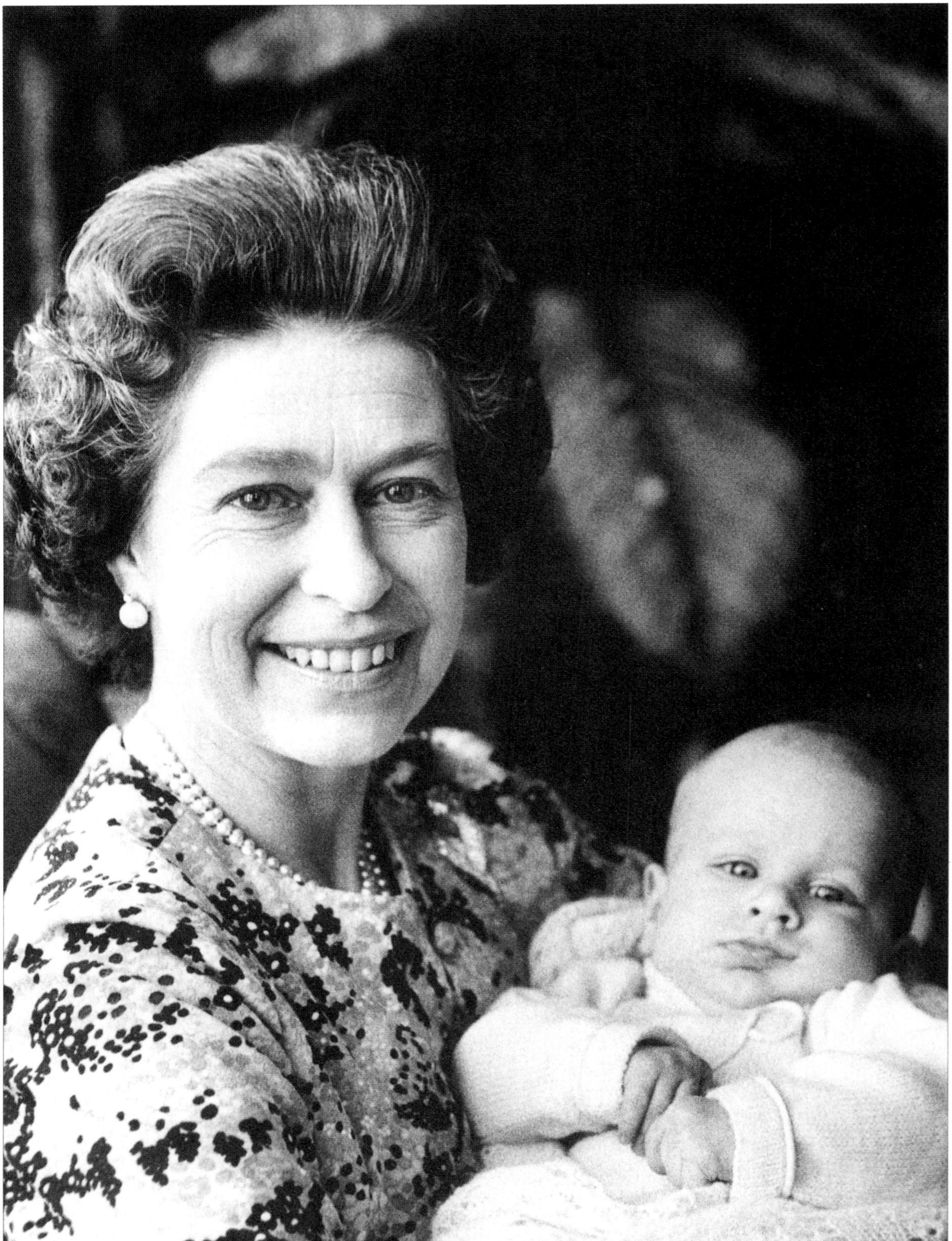

although Elizabeth II may be confidently expected to continue to reign over us for many more years yet, the forty-year mark provides us none the less with a good opportunity to offer her our congratulations, while looking back on the years since her accession in 1952 and trying to assess just how far they have brought us.

Thus the purpose of the exhibition is threefold: to celebrate, to inform and to take stock. First our central figure: who is she? To answer this question we have provided a family tree that traces her descent back almost exactly 1000 years to Ethelred the Unready, together with a series of photographs covering each year of her life up to 1952. On 6 February of that year, while she and her recently married husband were on an official visit to Kenya, the news was brought to her of the sudden death of the father she loved, King George VI. They returned immediately. Who can ever forget that famous picture of the small, black-clad figure emerging from the door of the aircraft while Sir Winston Churchill, Clement Attlee, Anthony Eden and others wait bare-headed at the bottom of the steps to receive her, their shoulders hunched against the winter wind?

On 2 June 1953, the Queen proceeded to her coronation. Here is the gown worn by her at the ceremony, together with her robe, gloves and prayer book, and the copes of the Archbishop of Canterbury and his fellow churchmen, while a video shows extracts from the original BBC television coverage. Elizabeth II has embarked on her life as Queen. A special section examines her roles as respectively Head of State, of the Church and of the Armed Forces and as Fount of Honour. We see her on visits to the Commonwealth, as well as to members of the European Community, the United States and elsewhere: by now there can be few leading statesmen anywhere in the world whom she has not met. Such luminaries she also receives on state visits to this country; and part of the Palace dining-table, set with gold plate, crystal and porcelain for a state banquet, produces one of the most dazzling displays in the exhibition.

The next section shows the astonishing development in the methods and approach of the press and television over four decades, and leads us up to the great video wall on which we follow the Queen's reign up to the present day, not only through its principal events but also in the daily life of her subjects. We then come to her wardrobe, which introduces us to the last room of the Exhibition and the more private aspects of the Queen's life. We look at her love of racing and, by way of contrast, at the Royal Collection, which she has made accessible through the Queen's Gallery. Thus we come at last to her life at home with the other members of the Royal Family. Here we have tried to evoke the atmosphere of the great royal country houses – Windsor, Sandringham and Balmoral – by re-creating a typical room in each.

How do we bring SOVEREIGN to an end? Elizabeth II is still Queen, and will surely remain Queen for as long as she lives. For crowned and anointed monarchs there can be no escape. Theirs is a life sentence, in which there are no holidays, no retirement. That is why we have chosen to close our exhibition without fanfares or any artificial grand climax, but on a quieter note: that of dedication, obligation and commitment – the continuing purpose.

John Julius Norwich

PRINCESS ELIZABETH

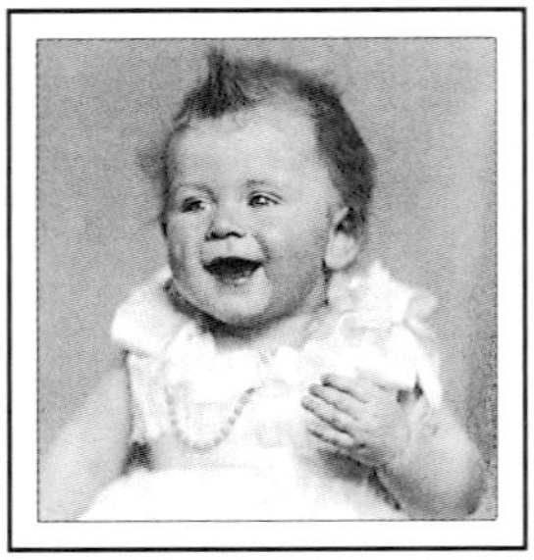

1926

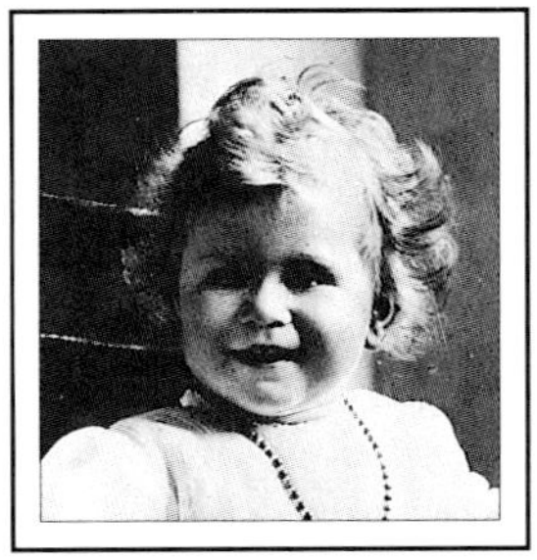

1927

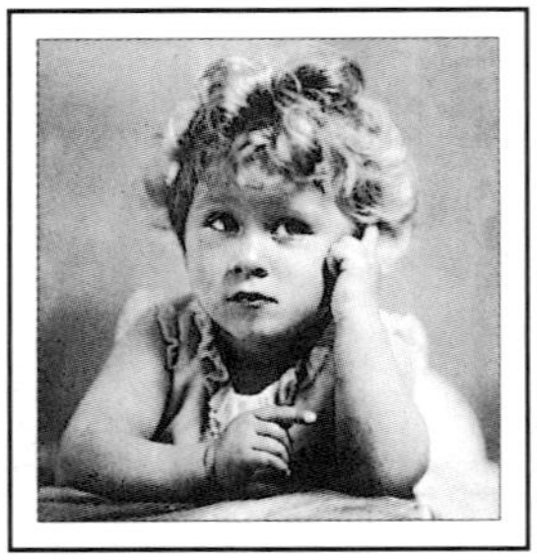

1928

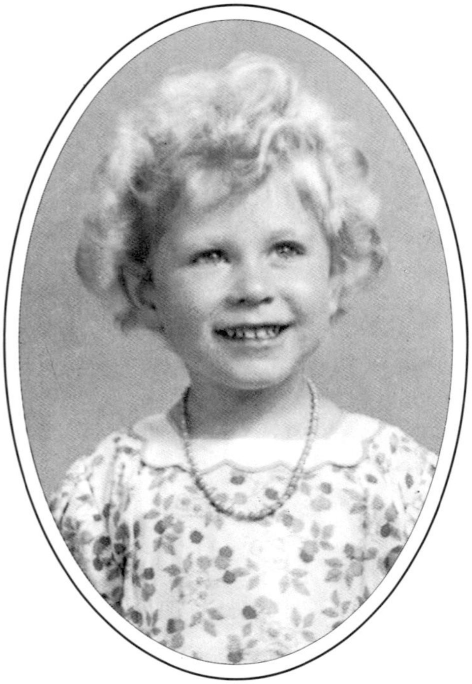

1929

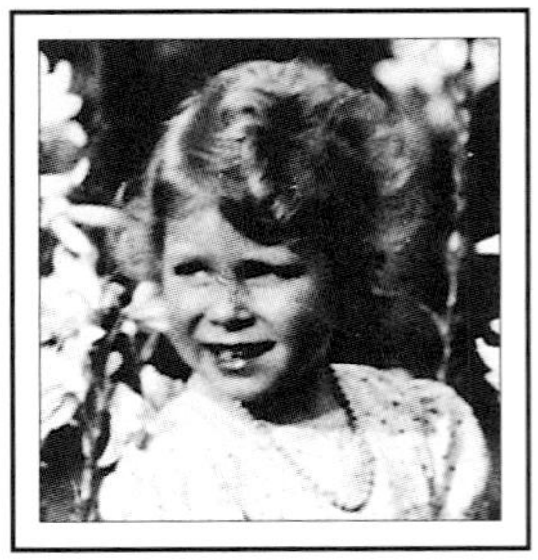

1930

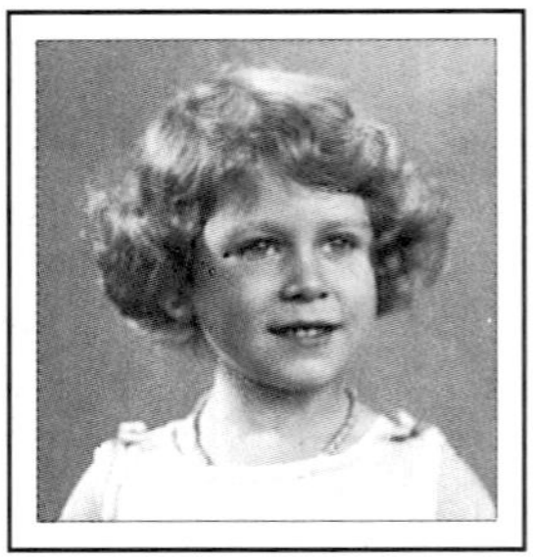

1931

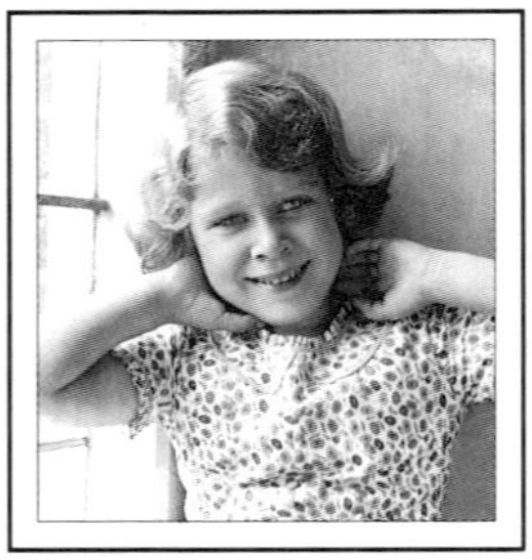

1932

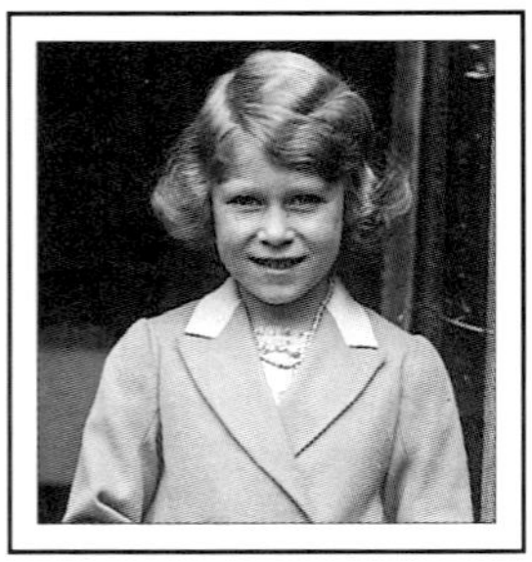

1933

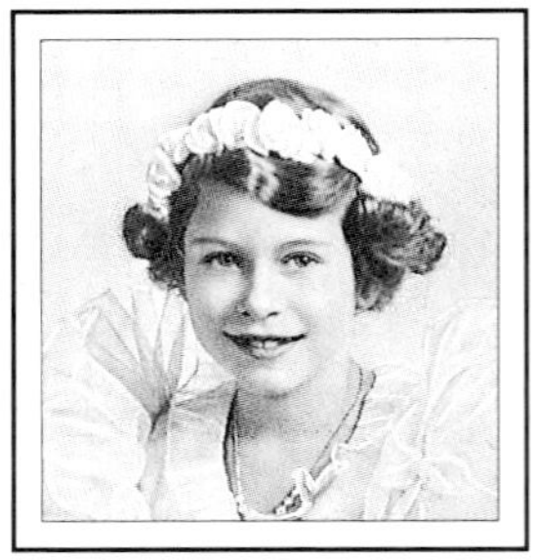

1934

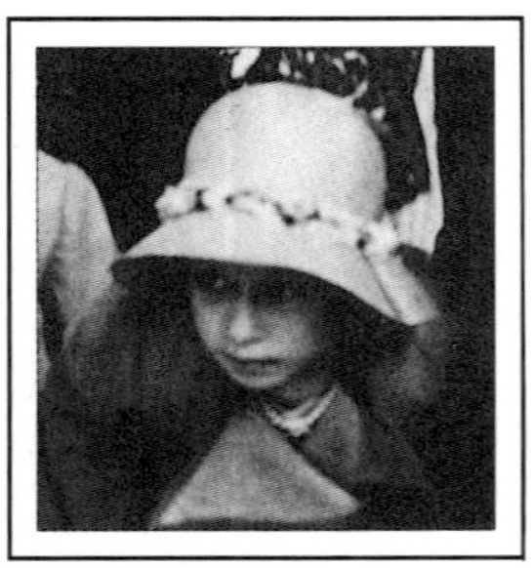

1935

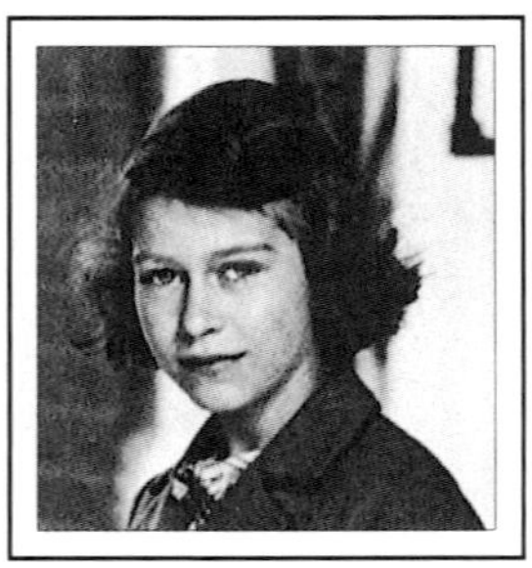

1936

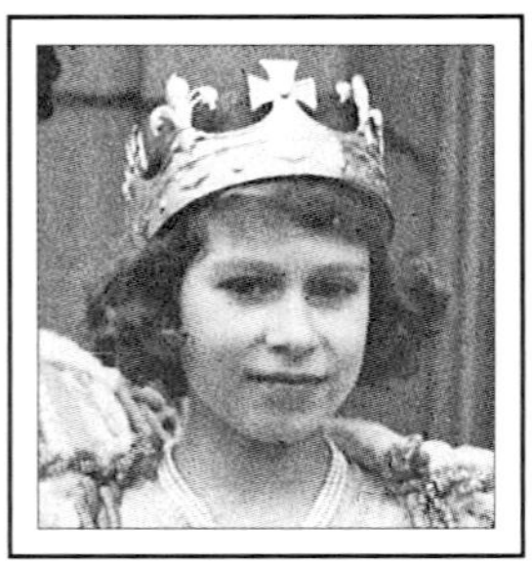

1937

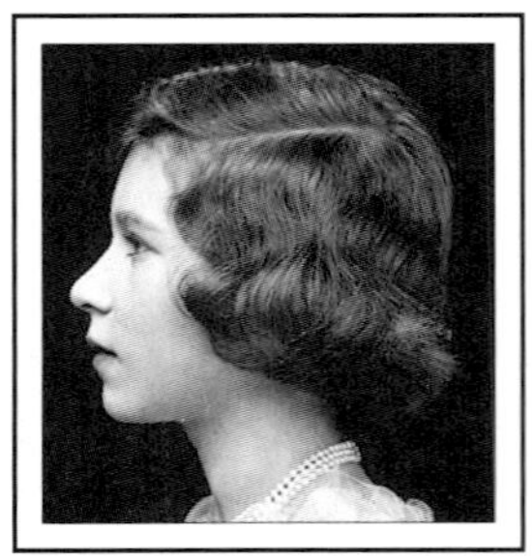

1938

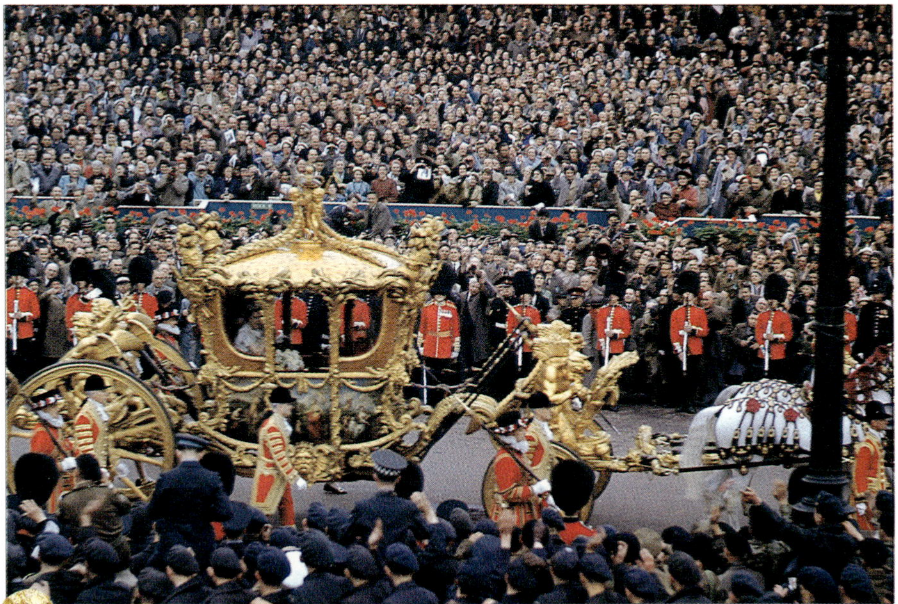

The Procession
The Queen travelled both to and from Westminster Abbey in the Gold State Coach. The coach was built in 1762 and weighs four tons. Eight horses draw the coach at walking pace.

The Coronation Coach
The exterior of the Gold State Coach is coated with gold leaf except for the panels painted by Giovanni Battista Cipriani. The structure consists of eight braces, shaped like palm trees. The roof is adorned with lions' heads and a crown supported by three cupids. Towards the front and back of the coach there is a pair of carved Sea Gods.

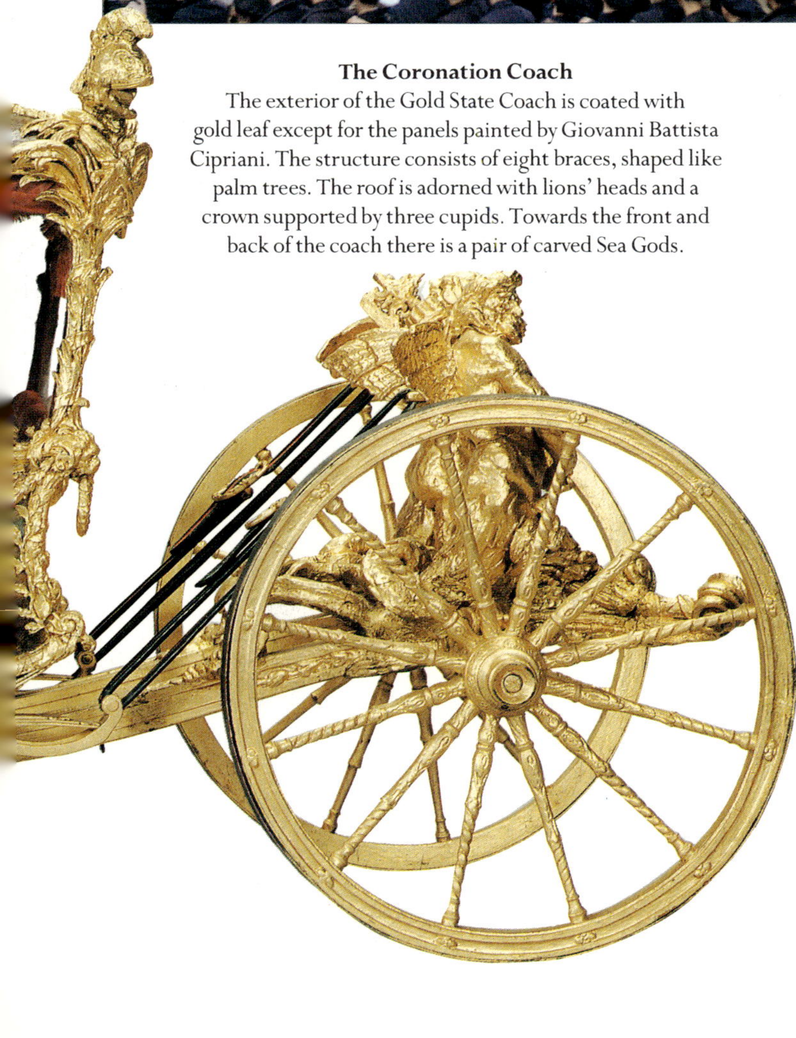

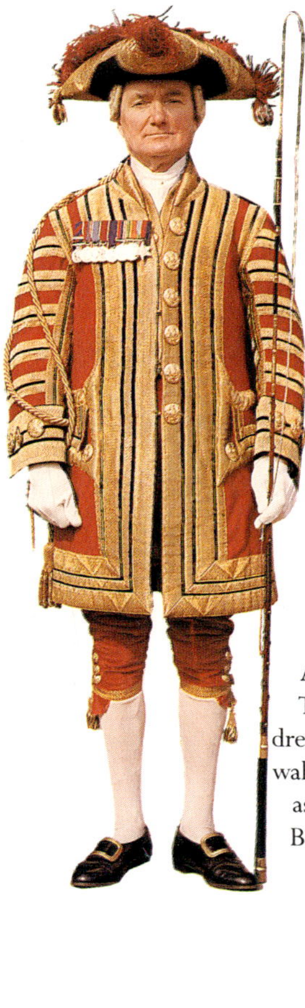

A Royal Coachman
The Royal Coachmen, dressed in Full State Livery, walked alongside the coach as it processed between Buckingham Palace and Westminster Abbey.

When the day dawned the crowds cheered everything that moved – starting with an early morning dustcart making a final clean sweep along the Mall. At last, shortly before 10.30 a.m., their vigil was rewarded with the first sight of the Gold State Coach. Its gilding glistened in the pouring rain of that English summer morning and inside, amidst the crimson satin of the interior, sat the Queen.

As the Queen entered the Abbey, over twenty million people, half the nation, watched on television: they had a better view than those guests who had waited for three hours in the Abbey.

The proceedings began with the recognition. Four times the Sovereign presented herself to the crowd in the Abbey: to east, to south, to west and to north. Four times the Archbishop of Canterbury declared, 'Sirs, I here present unto you Queen Elizabeth, your undoubted Queen. Wherefore all you who are come this day to do you homage and service, are you willing to do the same?'

Four times the response was returned with a roar: 'God save Queen Elizabeth!' The recognition was followed by the coronation oath, in which the sovereign pledges to rule lawfully and with mercy.

The coronation then continued with the anointing, the central and most sacred part of this religious ceremony, accompanied by the choir singing Handel's anthem 'Zadok the Priest'. Sitting in King Edward's Chair, under a canopy to shield her from general view, the Sovereign was anointed, blessed and consecrated by the Archbishop, who dispensed the oil from the seventeenth-century Ampulla.

Next came the investiture, for which the Queen put on a sleeveless white shift and a robe of gold cloth.

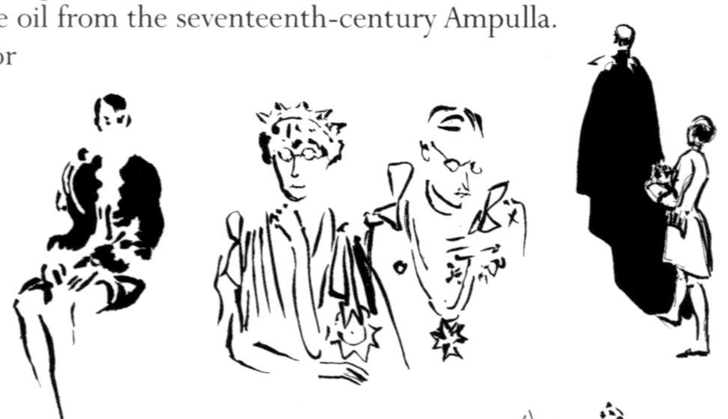

Coronation Sketches
While the coronation was in progress, Cecil Beaton took the opportunity to sketch the various characters and scenes that surrounded him.

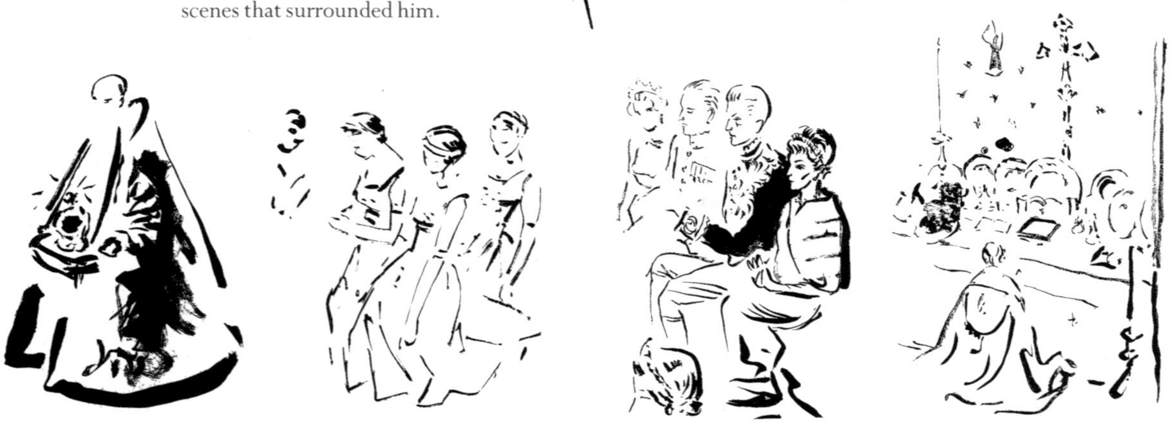

Cecil Beaton Portrait
The Queen is holding the Sovereign's Orb in her left hand, the Sceptre in her right. She is wearing the Imperial State Crown, her Hartnell-designed coronation dress, and the purple velvet Imperial Robe of State.

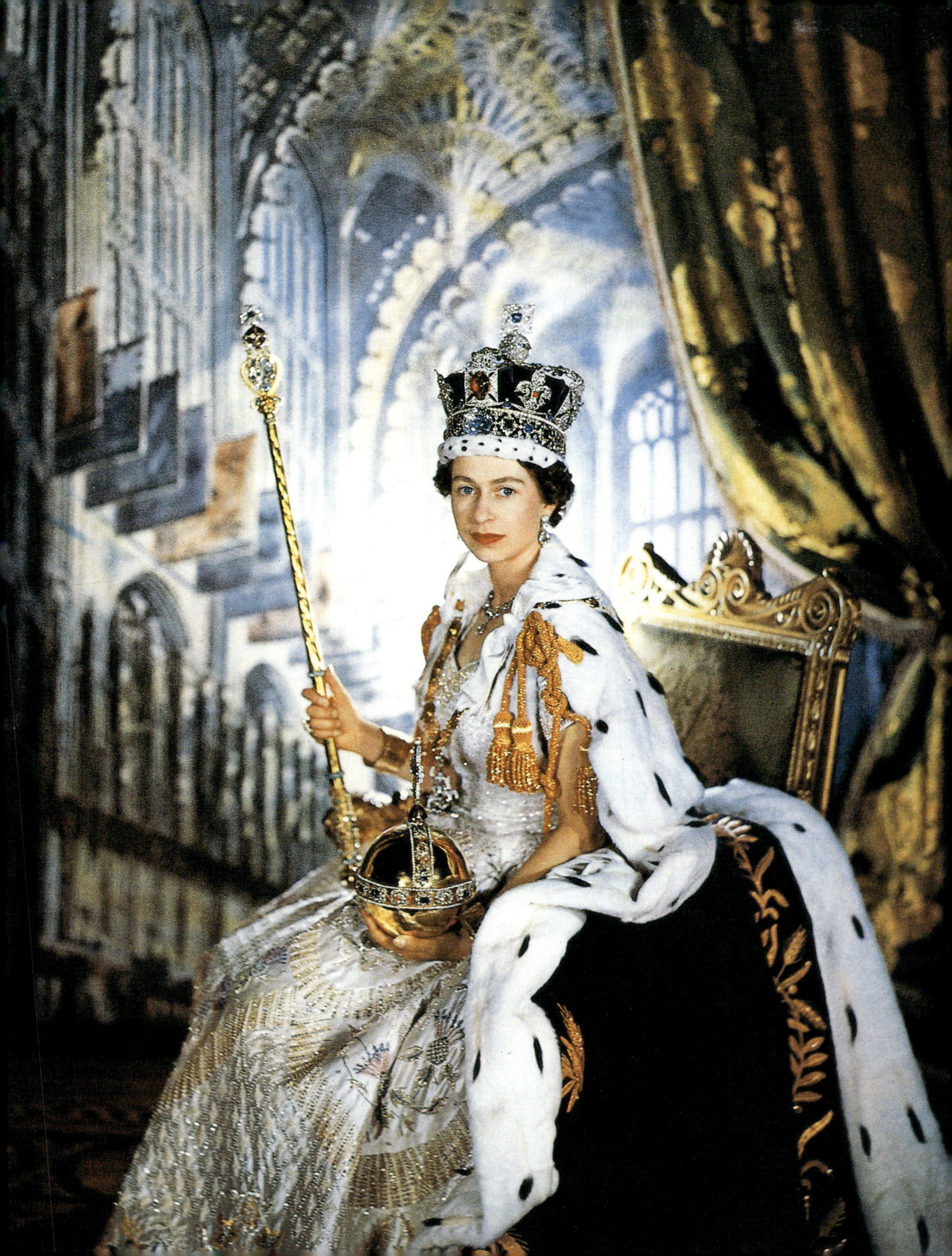

She was then presented with the golden spurs (symbols of chivalry), the jewelled sword and the armills – gold bracelets representing sincerity and wisdom.

After the Queen put on the royal robe, she received the orb and finally the coronation ring, the coronation glove, the sceptre with the cross and the sceptre with the dove. Thus bedecked she sat, motionless, for the crowning itself. The Archbishop then raised St Edward's Crown into the air and then, slowly and gently, lowered it on to the Queen's head. At this moment the peers and peeresses placed their coronets upon their own heads to ringing shouts of 'God Save the Queen!' and a fanfare of trumpets. Queen Elizabeth II moved to her throne to receive the homage; first from the Archbishop of Canterbury, from her consort (the Duke of Edinburgh), and then senior peers of the realm.

When the ceremonial was finished, the Queen took Holy Communion and withdrew to St Edward's Chapel. Here she changed into the Robe of Purple Velvet and exchanged the heavy St Edward's Crown for the lighter Imperial State Crown, before starting off on the return journey to Buckingham Palace.

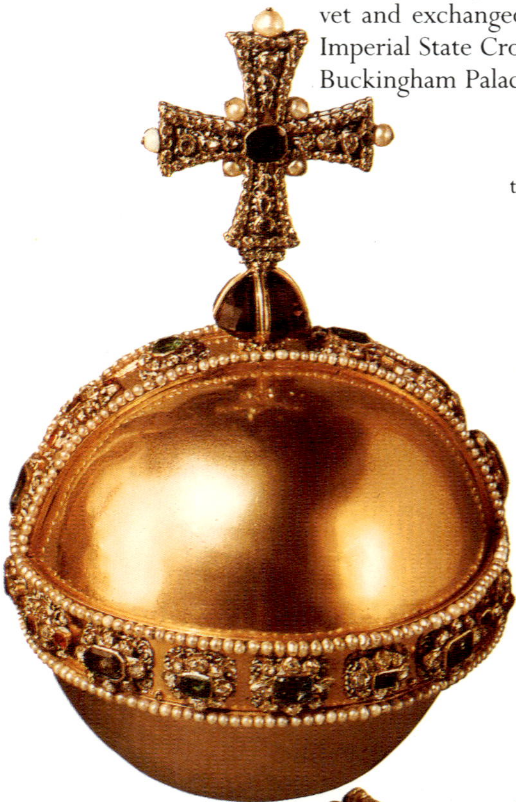

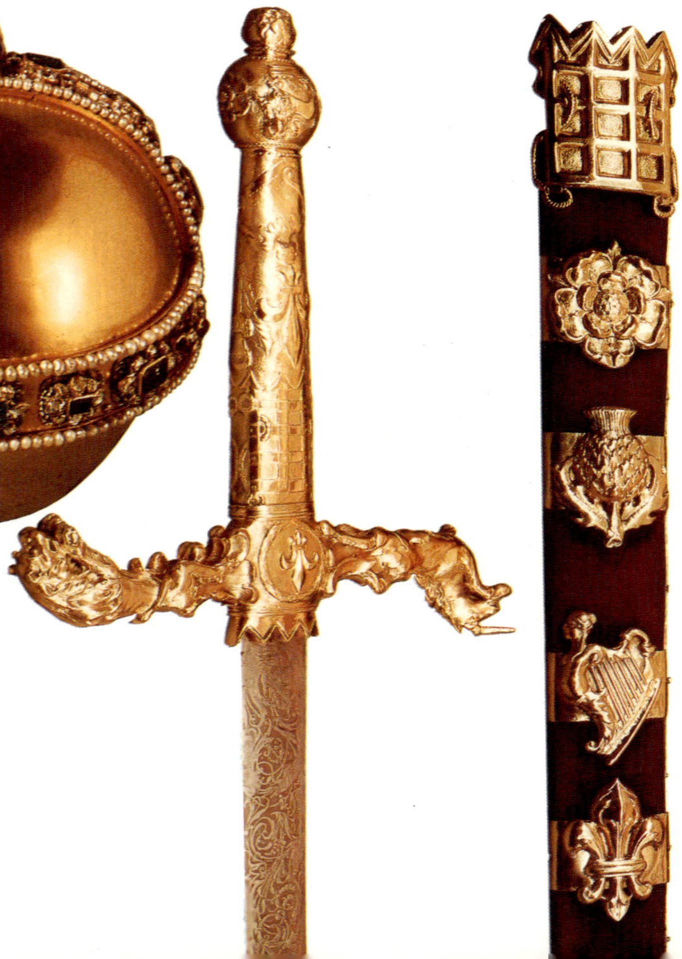

The Great Sword of State

This dates from 1678 and was first used at the coronation of James II. It symbolizes the sovereign's power and is used at the State Opening of Parliament.

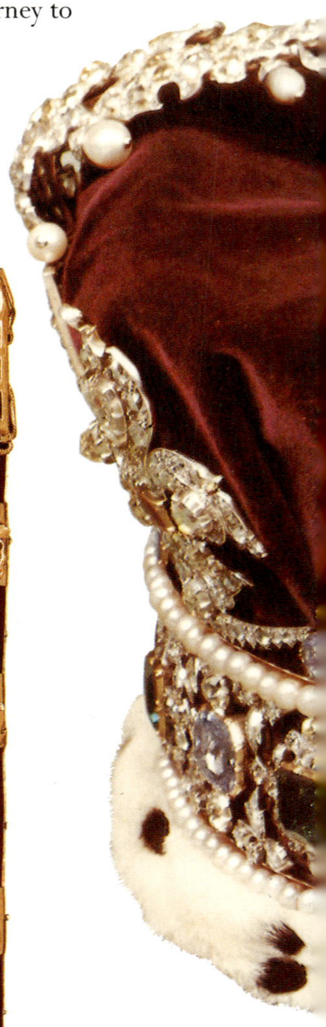

The Sovereign's Orb

The Orb, dating from 1661, was made for the coronation of Charles II. It is a hollow globe of gold, inset with rubies, sapphires and emeralds, which are surrounded by diamond clusters and bands of pearls. It is topped by a jewelled cross with an amethyst beneath.

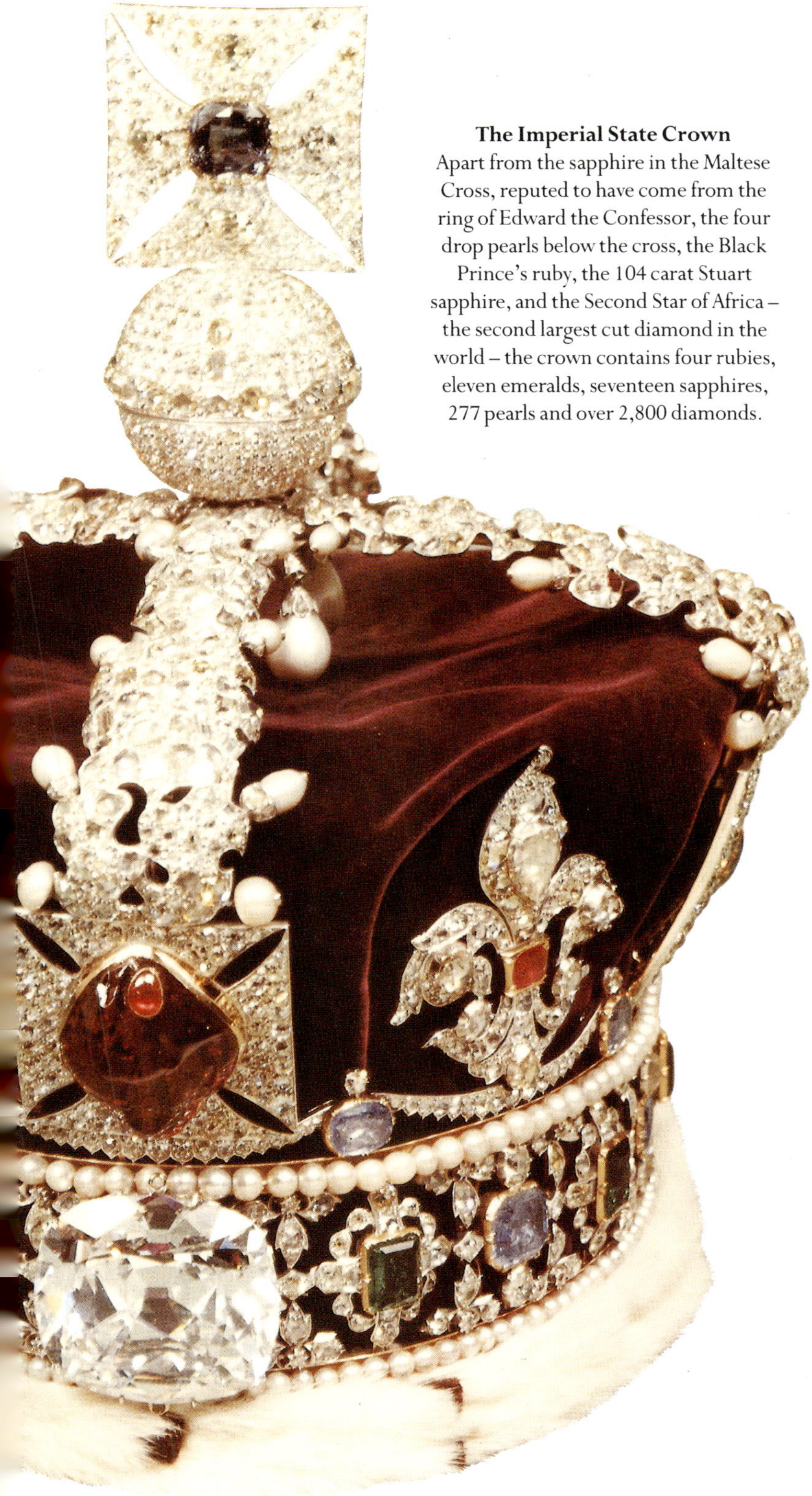

The Imperial State Crown
Apart from the sapphire in the Maltese Cross, reputed to have come from the ring of Edward the Confessor, the four drop pearls below the cross, the Black Prince's ruby, the 104 carat Stuart sapphire, and the Second Star of Africa – the second largest cut diamond in the world – the crown contains four rubies, eleven emeralds, seventeen sapphires, 277 pearls and over 2,800 diamonds.

The Sceptre with the Cross.
First created for the coronation of Charles II, the sceptre was remodelled in 1910 to receive the largest cut diamond in the world – the Star of Africa – which weighs 530 carats.

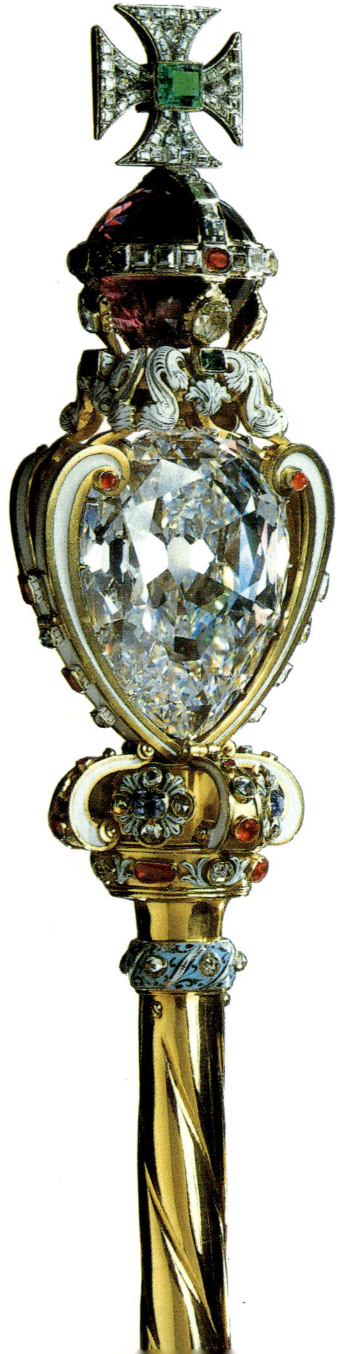

The CORONATION DRESS

THE WHITE SATIN DRESS HAD SHORT SLEEVES, a fitted bodice and a full skirt adorned with emblems. Its creator, Norman Hartnell, has described how the Queen was unwilling to wear a gown bearing emblems of Great Britain without those of other connected nations. Thus the dress bore Canada's maple leaf, Australia's wattle flower, New Zealand's fern, South Africa's protea, the lotus flower of India and Ceylon (now Sri Lanka), and for Pakistan the crops of wheat, cotton and jute. Each motif was superbly crafted and embellished with pearls, diamonds, amethysts, crystals and gold and silver sequins. To support such an abundance of heavy embroidery the skirt was lined with taffeta reinforced with horsehair so that it should hang properly, without any distortion to the emblems.

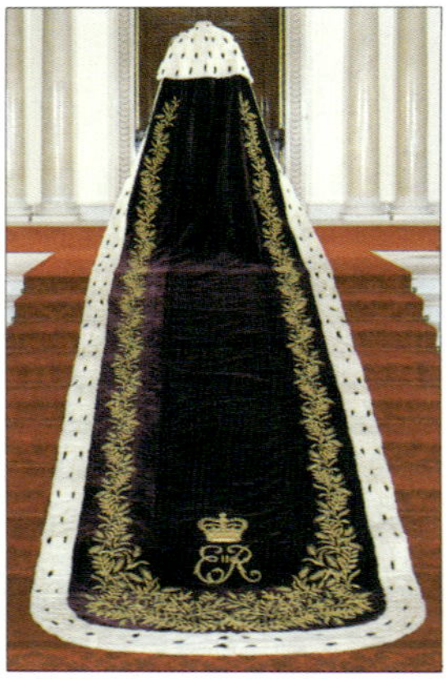

The Imperial Robe of State
The ermine cape, with its purple velvet train, is decorated with gold lace and filigree gold.

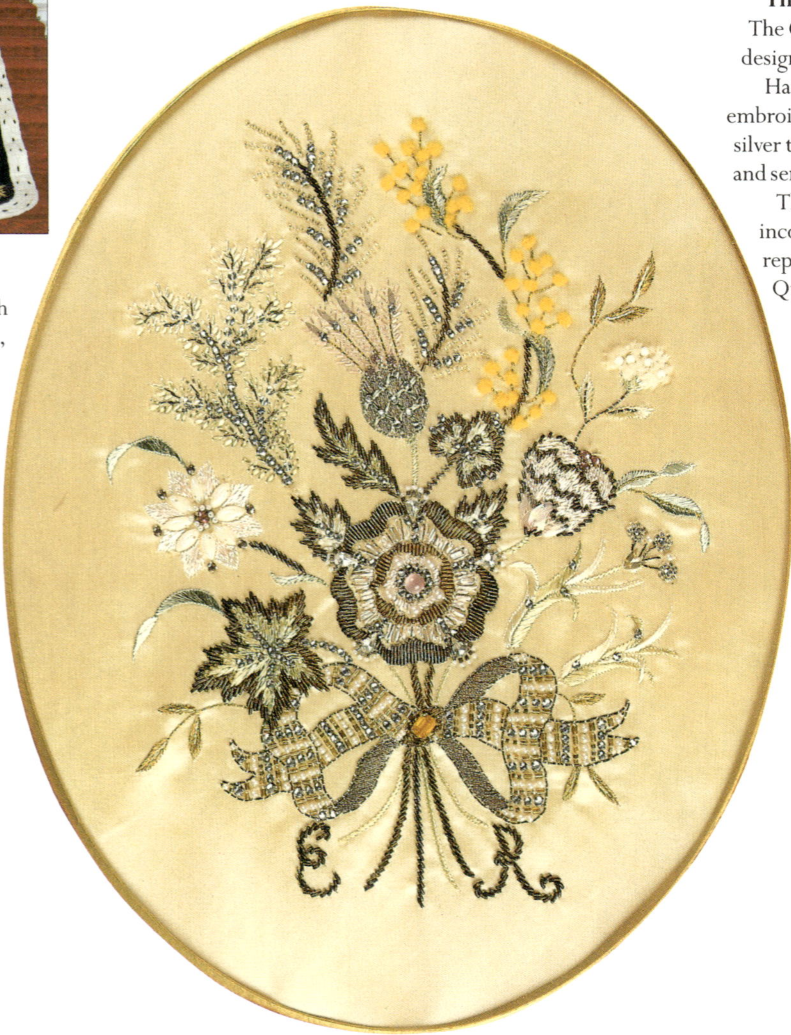

The Embroidery
The Coronation Dress designed by Sir Norman Hartnell was richly embroidered with gold and silver thread and precious and semi-precious jewels. The embroidery incorporated motifs representing all the Queen's dominions.

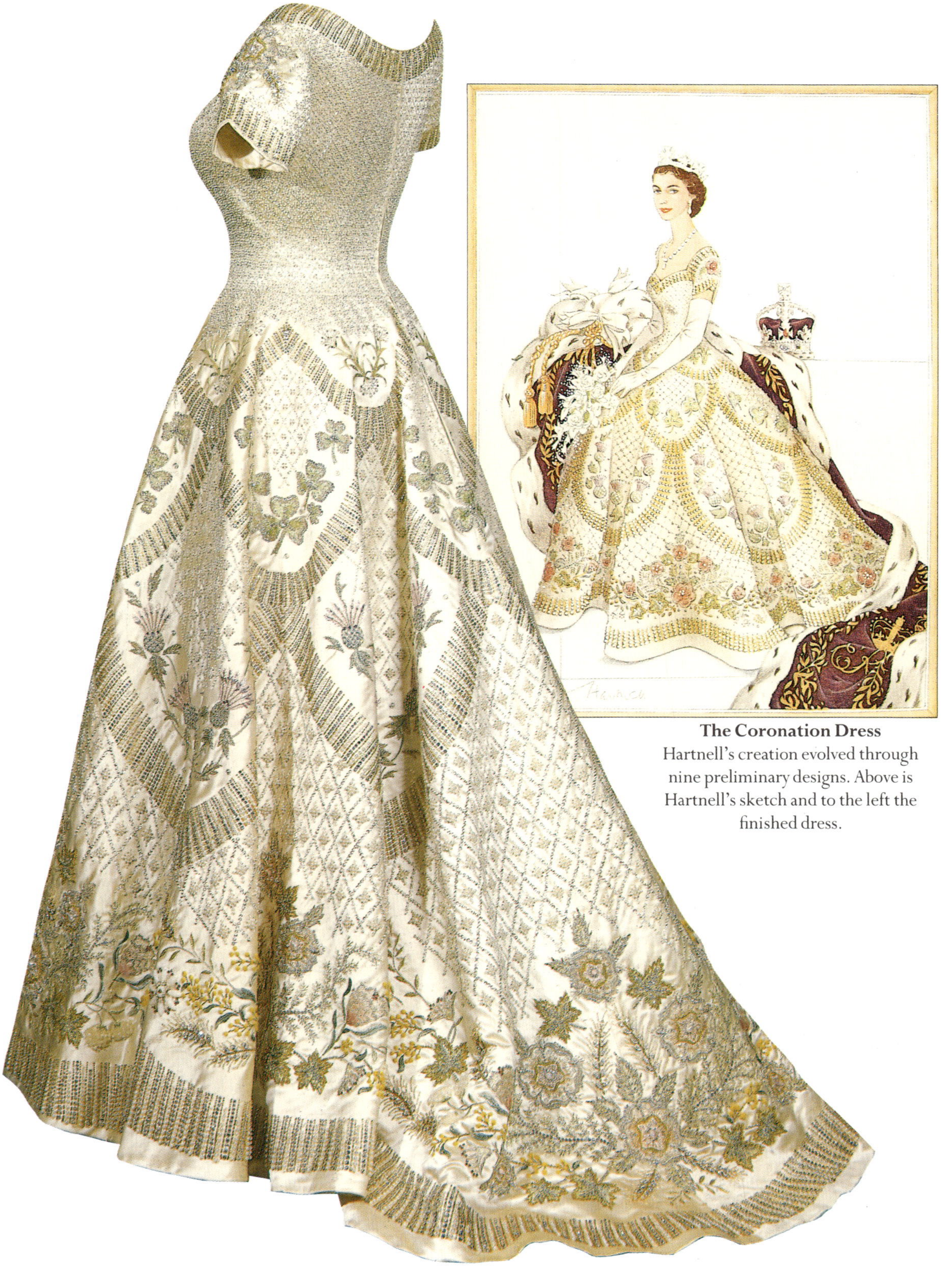

The Coronation Dress
Hartnell's creation evolved through nine preliminary designs. Above is Hartnell's sketch and to the left the finished dress.

A State Banquet

State visits between nations are a part of the world of international diplomacy. It would, of course, be unthinkable for the Queen to extend an invitation and be turned down. So the British Foreign and Commonwealth Office takes the first step in suggesting the overseas head of state to be invited and, if the Queen agrees, the suggestion is then explored unofficially with representatives of that country. Only when the reaction is positive is an official invitation issued.

The state banquet, usually given on the evening of the first day of the visit, either at Buckingham Palace or Windsor Castle, is an important public display of friendship or respect between the two nations.

The organization of such a banquet is formidable, especially as the word 'Royal' has become a synonym for excellence. Having a long tradition of ceremony

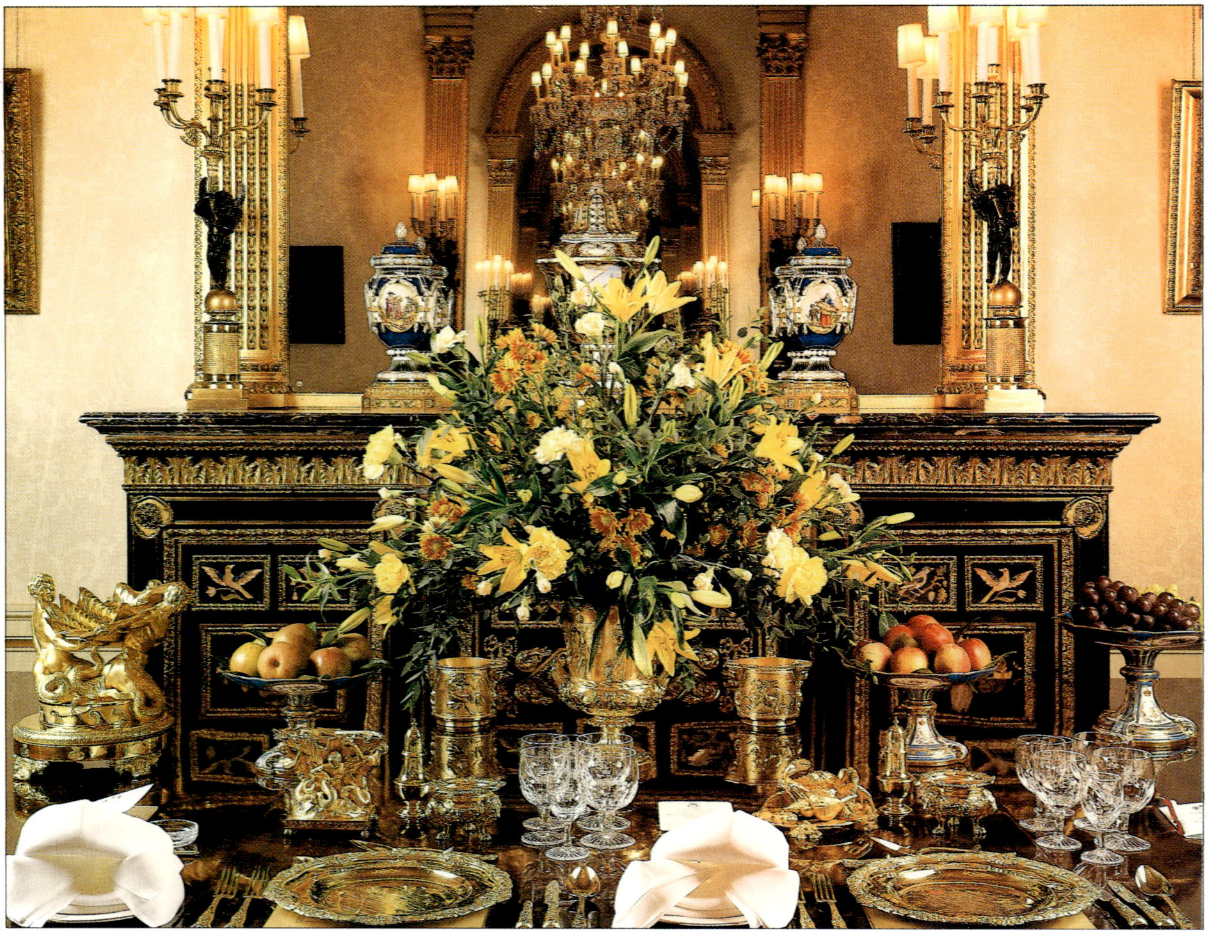

A Royal Banquet
A royal banquet is a carefully rehearsed occasion enhanced by flowers, music and, of course, magnificent ornaments.

is an advantage, however, in that the choreography remains essentially the same. A state banquet is a repeat performance with every detail honed to a fine art.

Nevertheless, each banquet takes several months of planning: from the preliminary discussions between the Master of the Household, Her Majesty's Private Secretary and the Foreign and Commonwealth Office about invitations, to the budget created by the Keeper of the Privy Purse – for the food, wine, music and decorations. The Yeomen of the Pantries are briefed as to the plate, glass and china to be used. It then takes a full two days just to lay the tables.

For a banquet at Buckingham Palace guests gather in the Picture Gallery, where they are received by the Queen and the visiting head of state, before taking their seats at the U-shaped dining-table in the Ballroom. Then all stand as the Queen's procession enters, led by herself and the visiting head of state, and preceded by both the Lord Chamberlain and the Lord Steward, walking backwards.

Menu and Seating Plan
A banquet in honour of Lech Walesa and his wife. With quails' eggs for first course, the place setting would have varied slightly from that pictured below.

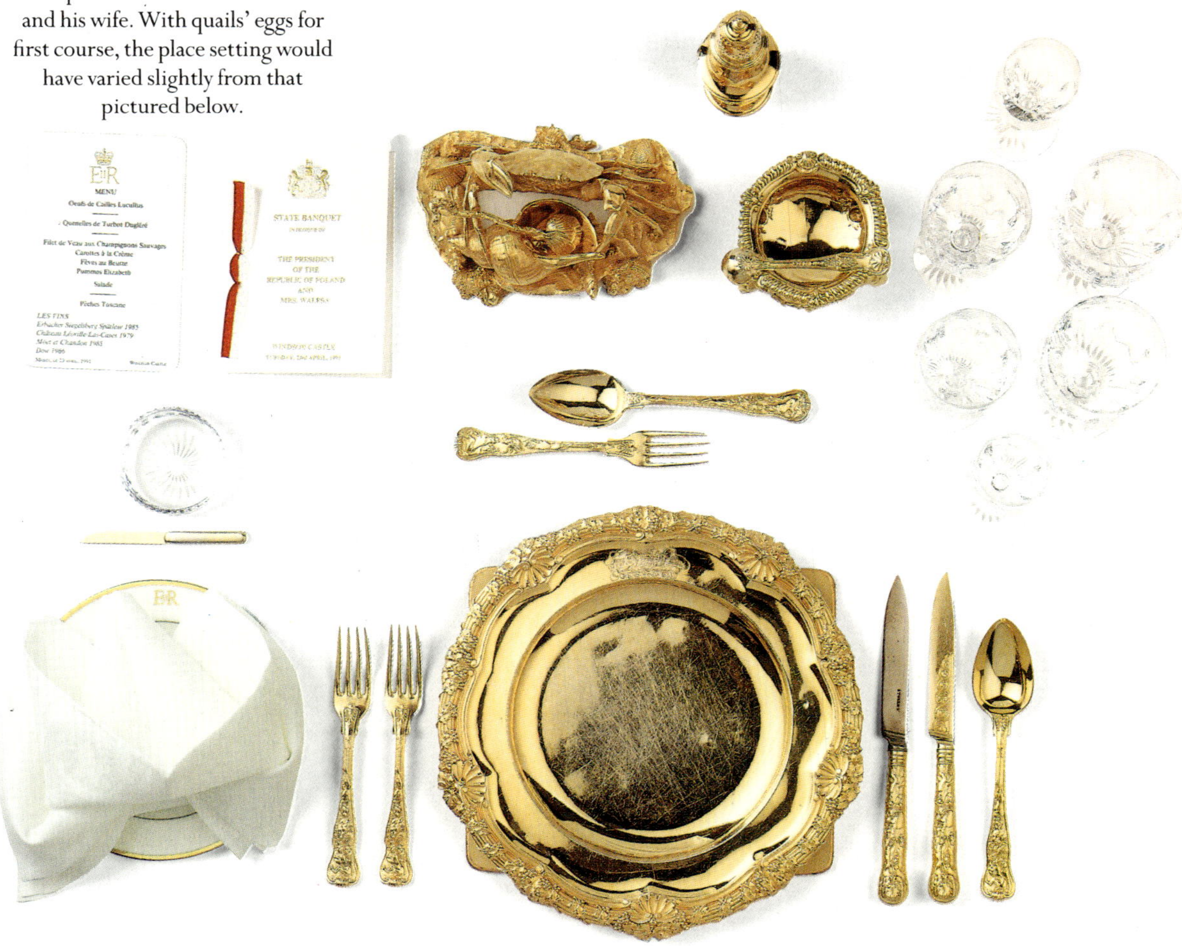

A Banquet Setting
The table setting is for four courses – soup, fish, meat and dessert. There are one glass for sherry, three for wine, one for water and one for port.

The Queen, her principle guests and other members of her procession sit at the top of the U-shaped table, while the remaining 160 or so guests are distributed according to a seating plan finely tuned to the nuances of diplomacy and rank. Guests are waited upon by footmen in a livery of scarlet and gold, assisted by pages in black and gold.

At the end of dinner the Queen makes a speech, to which the visiting head of state replies, and proposes the Queen's health. Then twelve pipers enter and march around the table before playing a strathspey and reel. They then perform another march around the table and exit. The Queen and her procession then leave as they entered, followed shortly afterwards by the other guests, who withdraw to a nearby State Room for coffee and liqueurs.

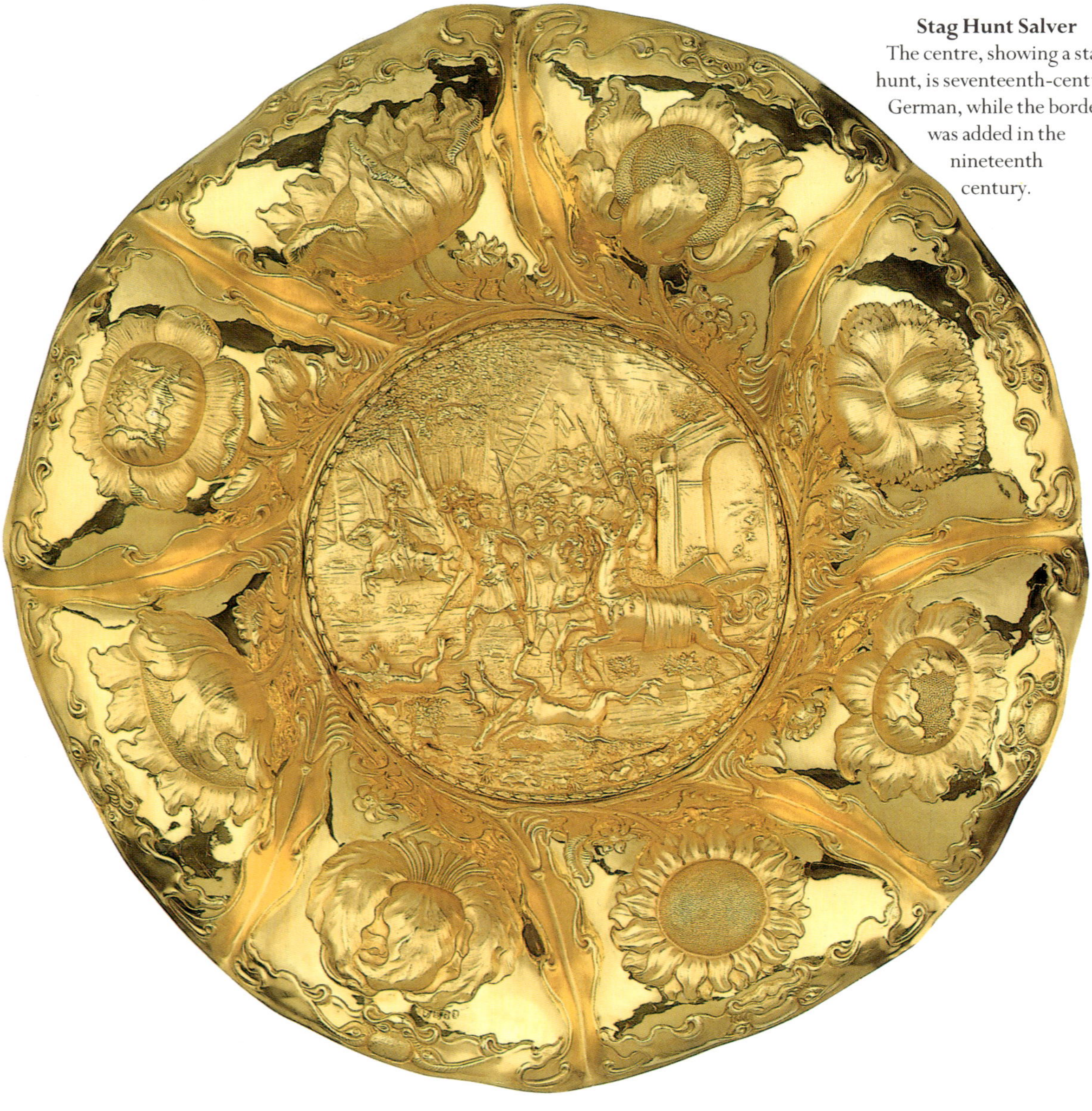

Stag Hunt Salver
The centre, showing a stag hunt, is seventeenth-century German, while the border was added in the nineteenth century.

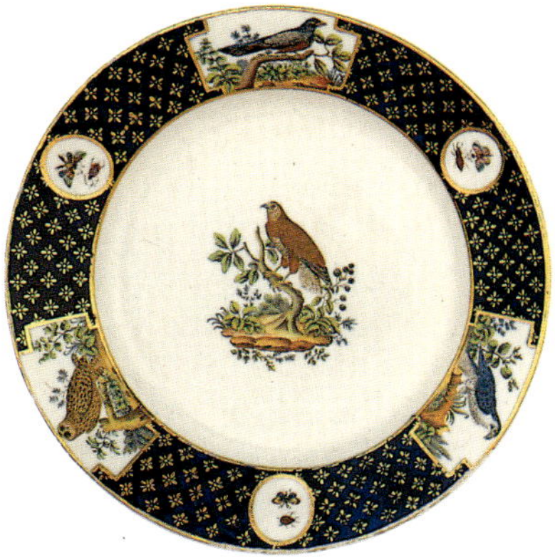

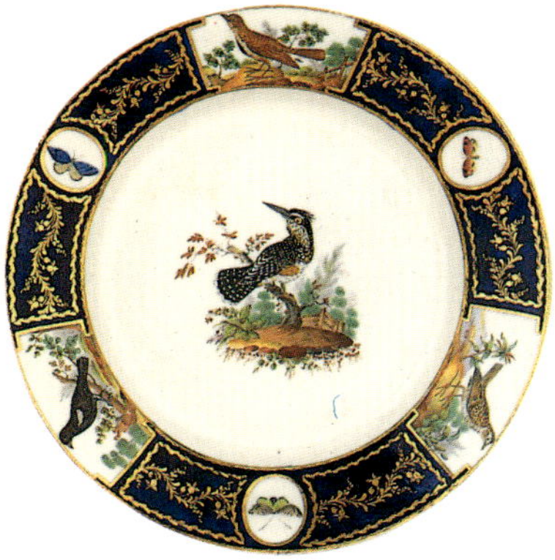

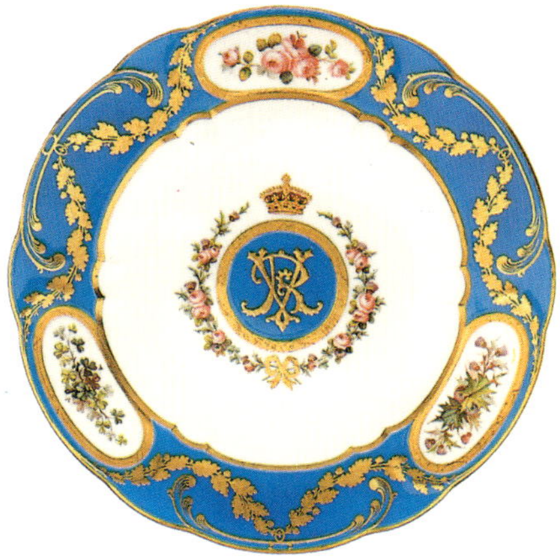

Tournai Porcelain
These two delightful plates (above and left) were part of a service of 1,603 pieces – now dispersed – commissioned in 1787 by Philippe, Duc d'Orléans.

Minton
This plate is from a service commissioned from the Minton factory by Queen Victoria.

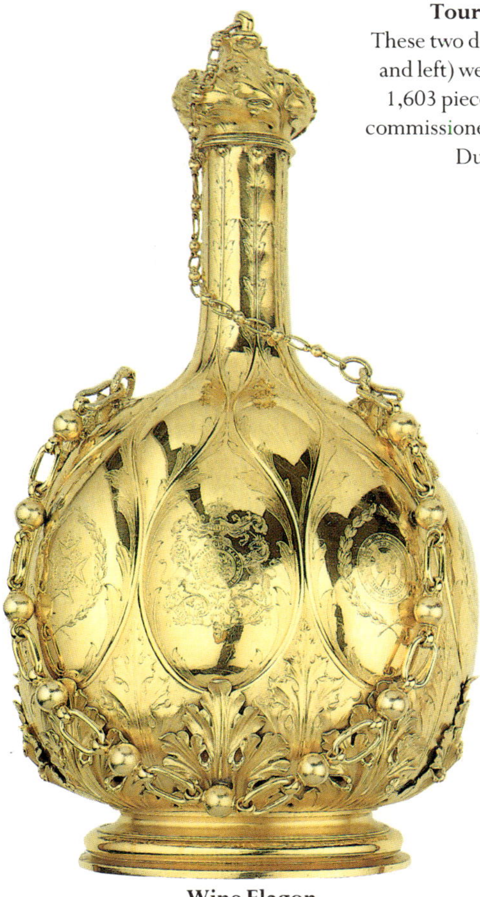

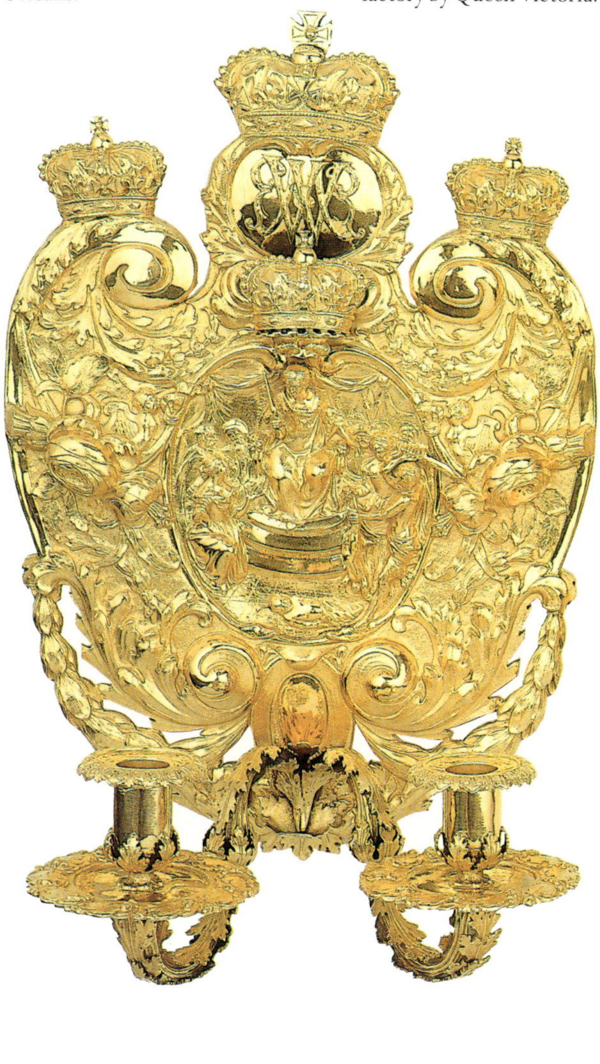

Wine Flagon
This richly chased flagon (above) incorporates the emblems of England, Scotland and Wales. It was made by John Bridge in 1828.

Candle Sconce
The relief on this sconce (right) depicts the Judgement of Solomon.

DRESSING TO BE SEEN

THE QUEEN, IT IS SAID, does not judge people by their dress, but by whether they are neat and tidy. She is also reported as being largely indifferent to fashion, and when pursuing her private outdoor interests she is most likely to be wearing a waterproof jacket and a headscarf. None the less, her varied and numerous public engagements mean that she takes her choice of clothes seriously as a practical element in doing her job. After all, many more people see the Queen from a distance than have an opportunity to talk to her, and she wants her clothes to enhance their view of her.

The Queen has steered a careful sartorial line – neither drab nor ostentatious. Where the occasion warrants it and expectations are not to be dashed, she will commission a special garment. Her designers have included Sir Norman Hartnell, Sir Hardy Amies, Ian Thomas and John Anderson. They, together with the Queen's dresser – Margaret 'Bobo' MacDonald – have created her style.

This style is a mixture of 1950s and 1970s fashion. Some people have observed that had the Queen had a French rather than an English dresser, then she would have been a leader of fashion. But in modern times it is not appropriate for heads of state to be fashion plates, and in any case the Queen has developed her own style – consistent but not boring.

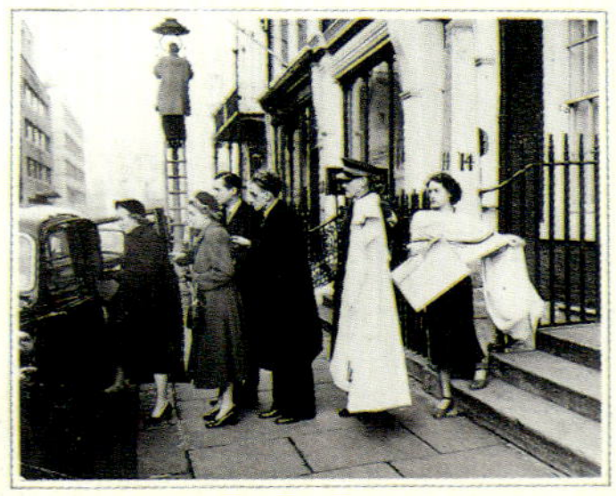

Betty Reeves, Maud Beard, Hardy Amies, Mr. Leonard setting off for Buckingham Palace 1954

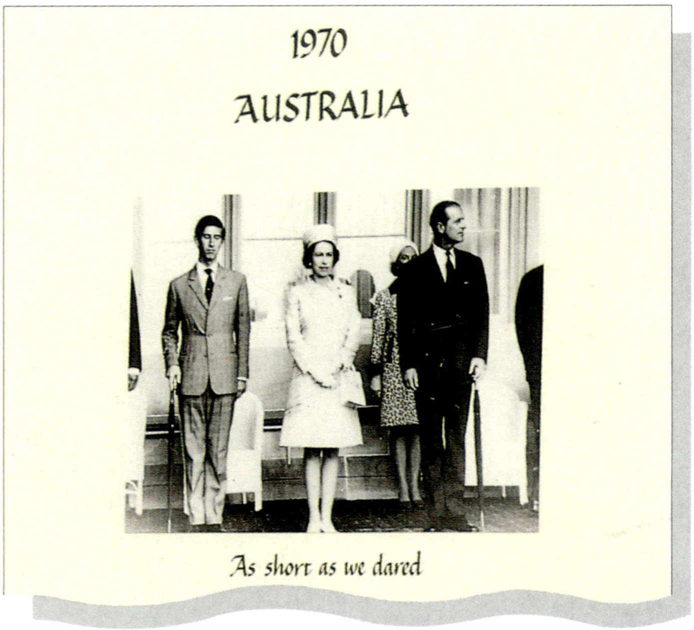

Modern but Modest

Hardy Amies had shortened his Sovereign's dress as far as he dared.

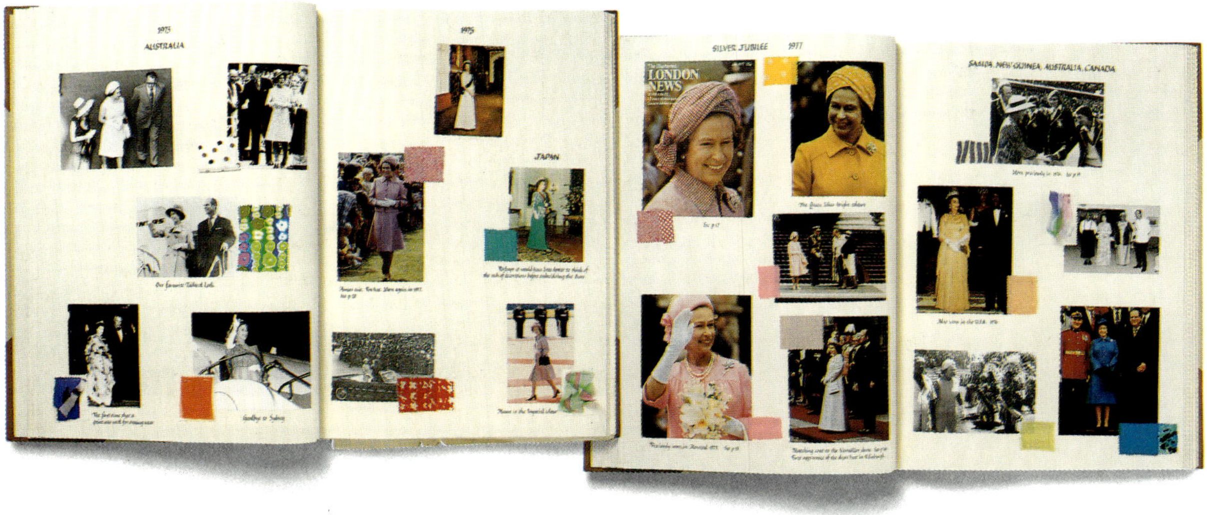

The Albums
After each royal tour Hardy Amies and his staff compiled a scrapbook of photographs and press cuttings of the Queen in her various outfits, which they then annotated. Shown here are pages featuring the Australia tour of 1973, Japan in 1975, the Queen's Silver Jubilee tour in 1977 and her visit to the USA in 1983.

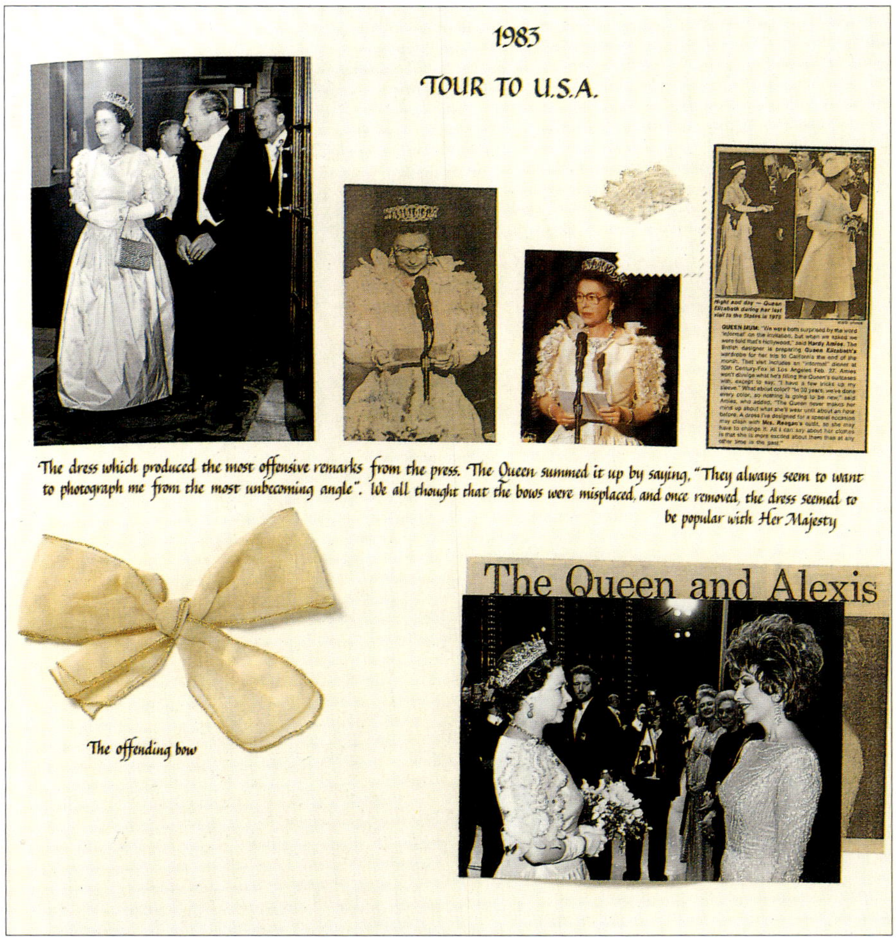

Simply by being who she is the Queen creates an effect of subdued drama and this is often heightened by the vivid colours she wears. The Queen likes bright colours which make her stand out; she is fortunate because her colouring allows her to wear difficult hues such as yellow and lime green.

Her clothes have to be comfortable, suitable for the occasion and easy to change. A designer who is given a brief for, say, a royal tour is expected to provide appropriate changes of clothing that take account of the different climates to be encountered. Drawings are submitted to the Queen with full portraits to show the total effect. A visit to the Palace is normally made with further sketches and fabric samples and the Queen usually takes two or three days to consider the suitability of the designs – and the costs. The Queen is not parsimonious in providing clothes for 'the job' but she is also not profligate and outfits are often worn many times.

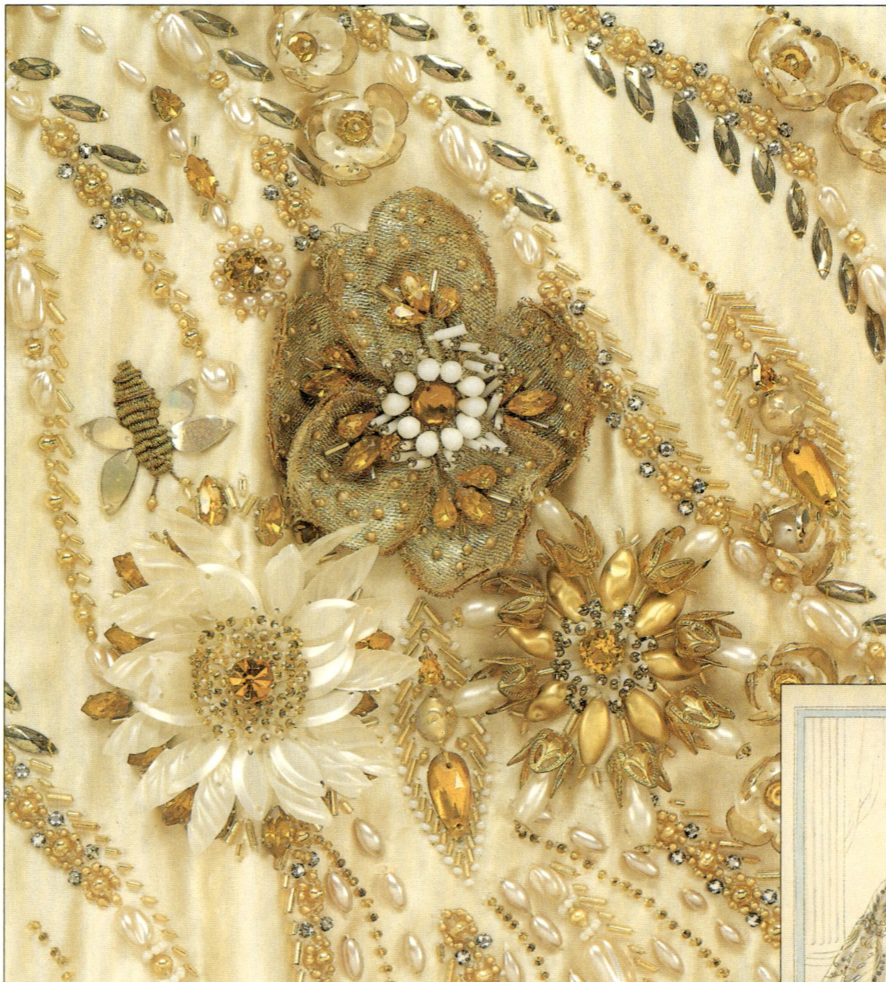

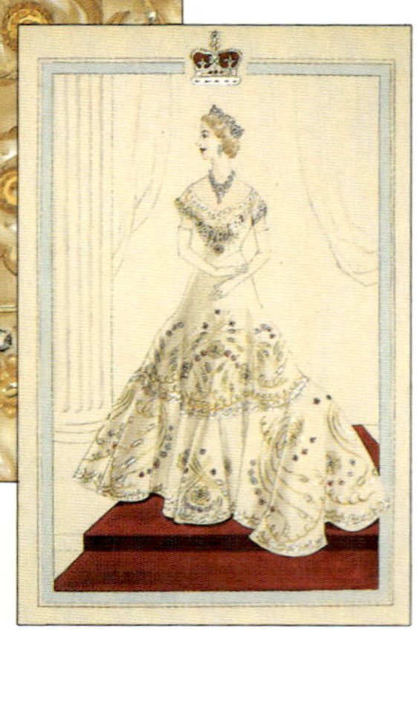

Norman Hartnell
This embroidery was for the State Evening Dress sketched right, first worn by the Queen in 1957.

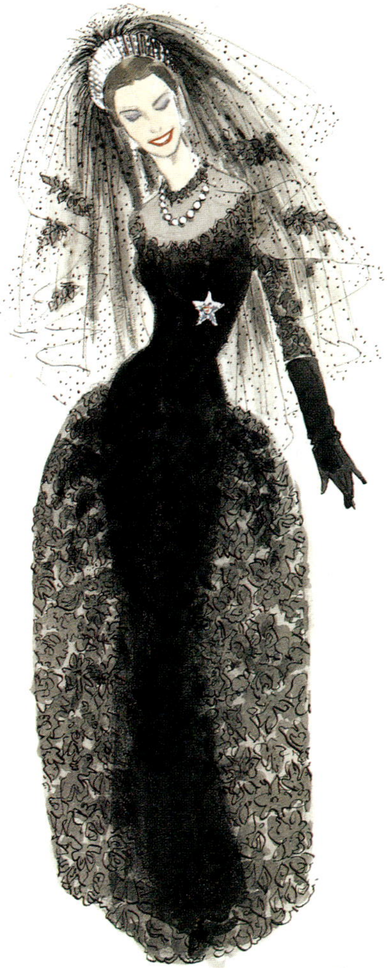

Norman Hartnell
The beautiful lace dress to the left was designed for the Queen's visit to the Vatican in 1961. The lace is mounted on stiff net, and flowers from the lace were appliquéd round the black-net yoke and edged the black tulle veil. The white dress to the right, embroidered with silver thread, diamonds and emerald drop beads, was for Iran, 1961. Below, with samples attached, are sketches for day outfits, prepared for the Queen's approval.

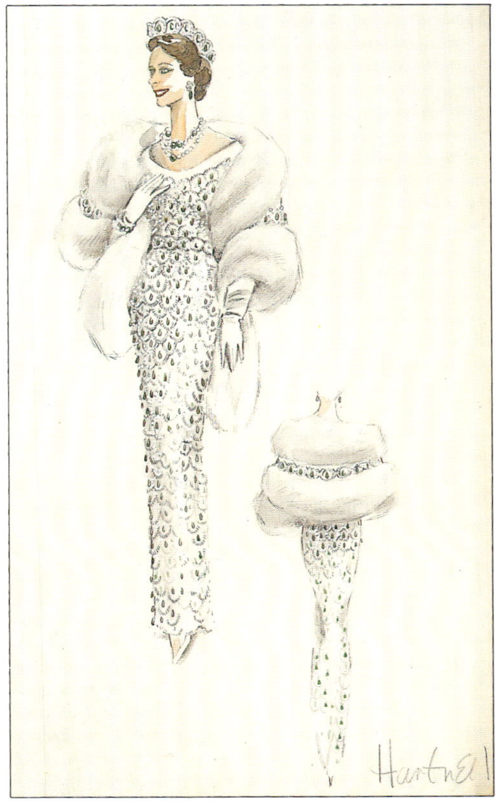

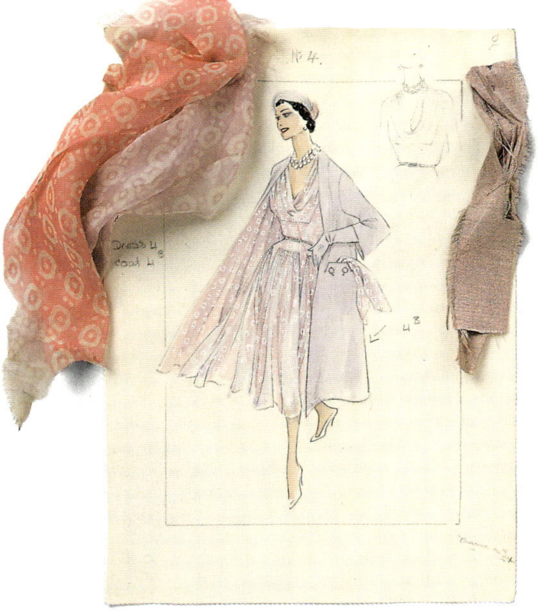

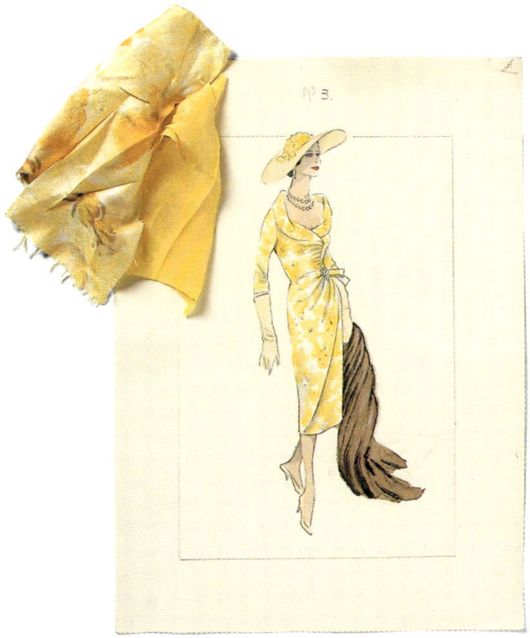

PLAN OF THE EXHIBITION

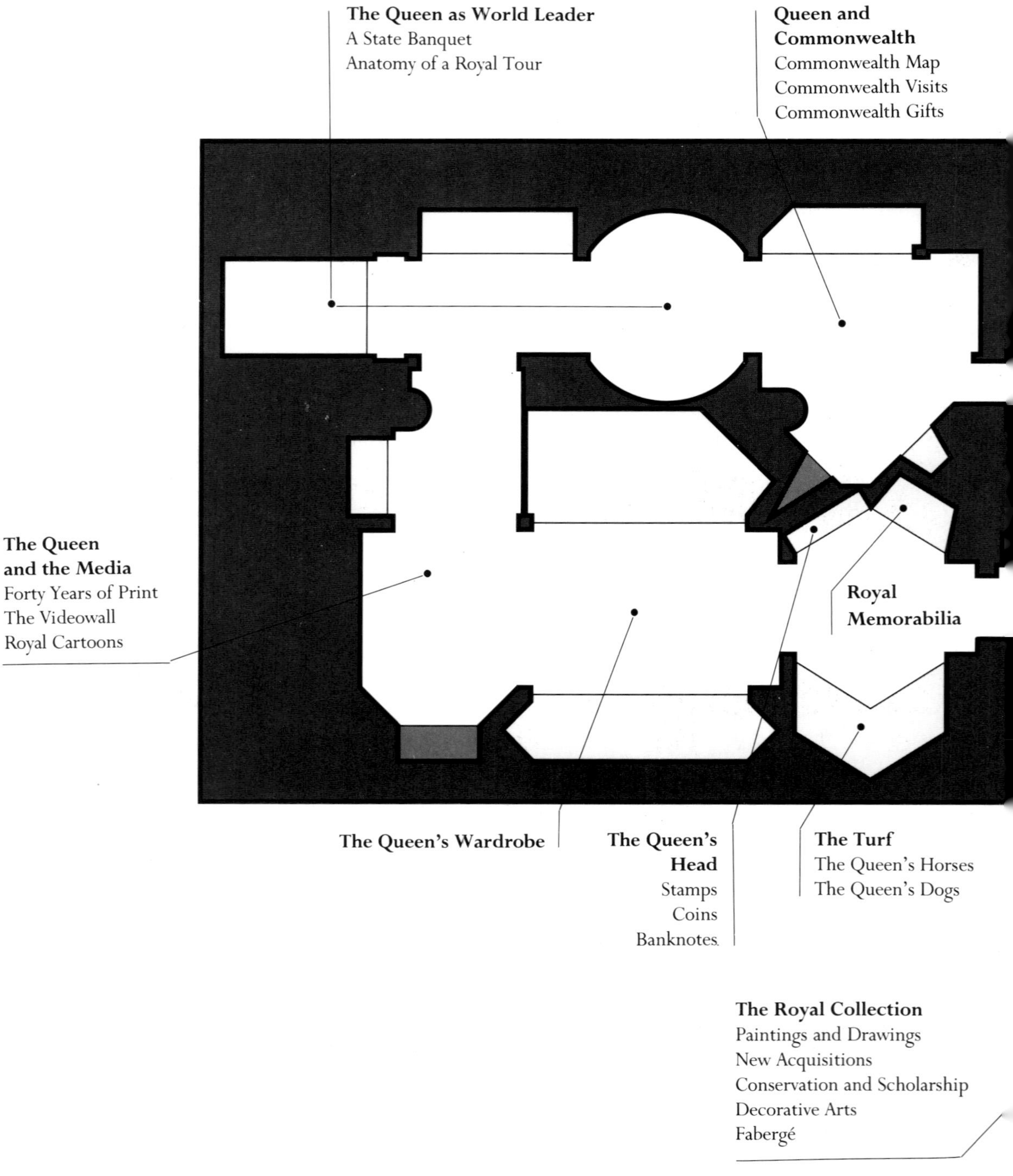

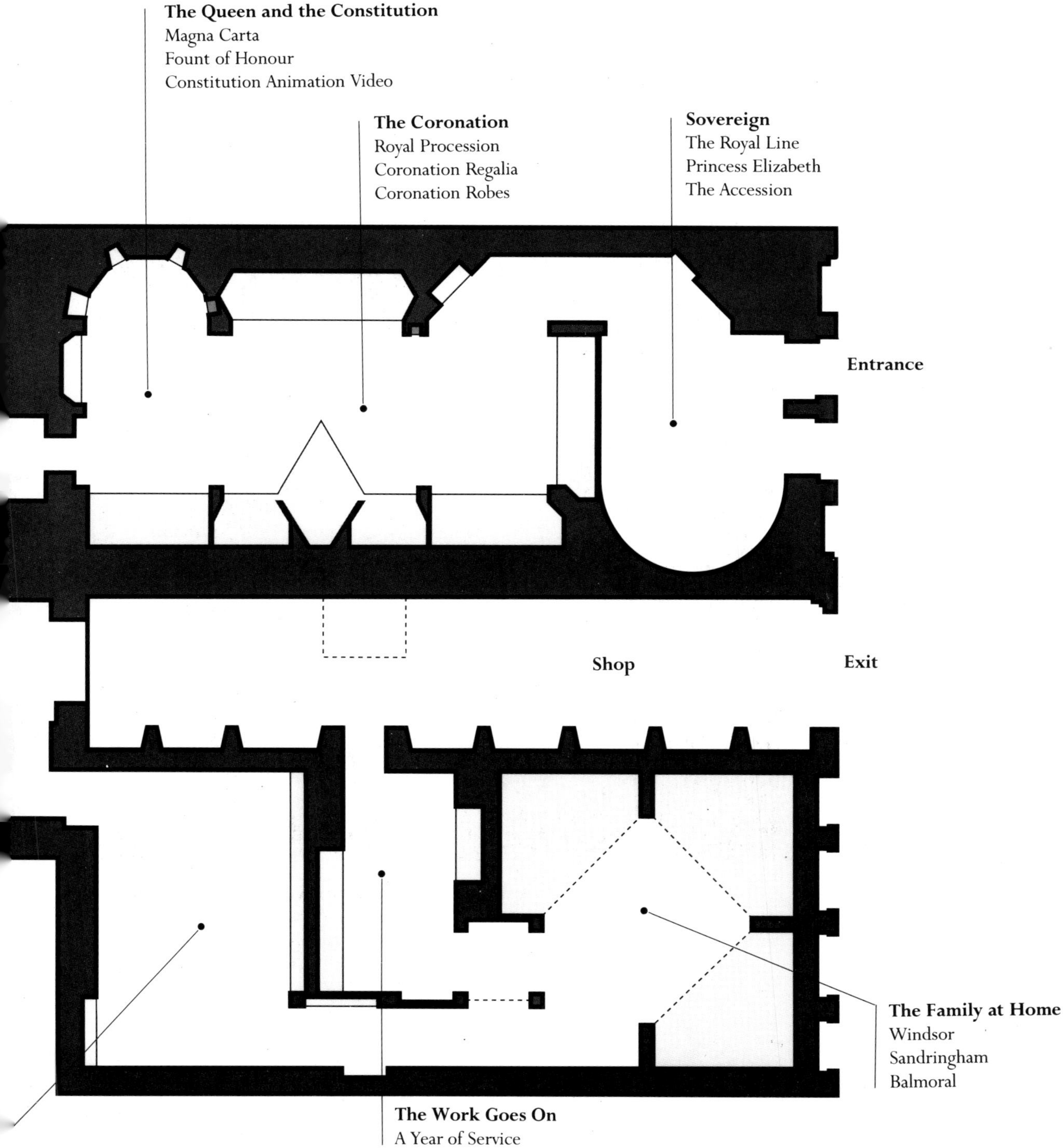
The Queen and the Constitution
Magna Carta
Fount of Honour
Constitution Animation Video
The Coronation
Royal Procession
Coronation Regalia
Coronation Robes
Sovereign
The Royal Line
Princess Elizabeth
The Accession
Entrance
Shop
Exit
The Family at Home
Windsor
Sandringham
Balmoral
The Work Goes On
A Year of Service

ROYAL MEMORABILIA

CERAMIC FIGURES AND DECORATED MUGS, plates and jugs, marking the coronation of monarchs and other royal occasions, have been produced by British potteries since the middle of the seventeenth century. Although design purists might raise their eyebrows at certain examples, the popularity of the genre with the public increases with every new event.

No official mugs were produced for the 1953 coronation, but this did not stop hundreds of thousands of mugs, cups, plates and tins from flooding the market. The prices they fetch today naturally vary according to the quality of the workmanship and, of course, their degree of rarity.

Some items of memorabilia have become both collectors' items and shrewd investments. For while it is true that run-of-the-mill mugs commemorating the coronations of Edward VII, George V and George VI are still cheap, those celebrating that of Queen Victoria can now fetch in excess of £1,000. Many mugs were also produced in anticipation of the coronation of Edward VIII, which of course did not happen, and now possess a certain curiosity value. Those actually marked 'Abdication' are much rarer and therefore more valuable.

Lidded Pot
This unusual pot is one of a limited edition of 200 made by Adderley China.

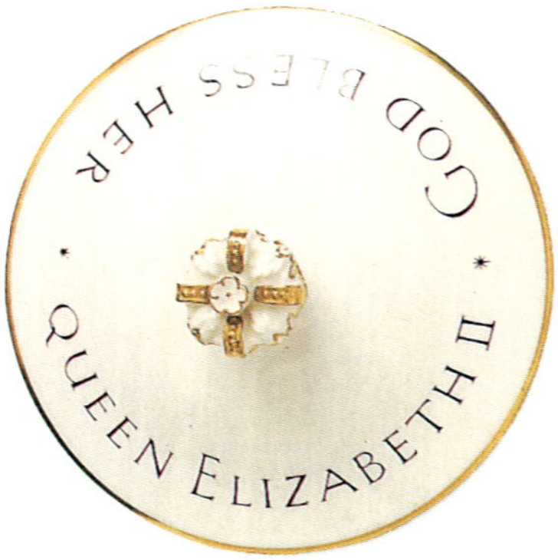

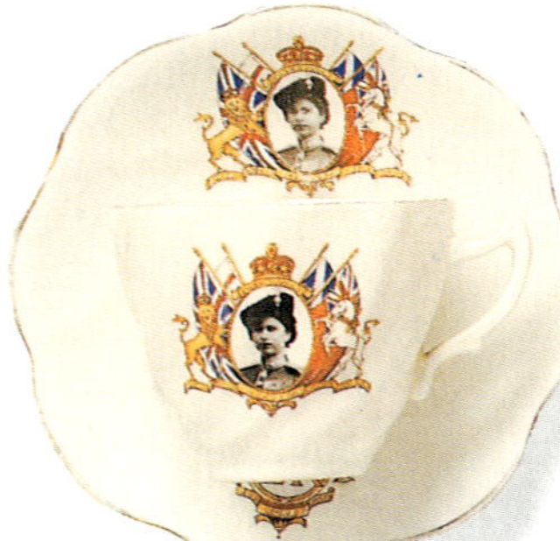

Tea-cup and saucer
Coronation bone china made by Rosina.

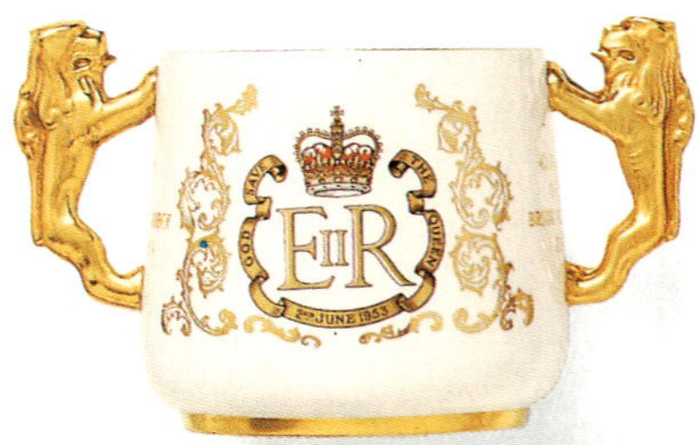

Loving Cup
It shows the royal coat of arms on the reverse side and was made by Paragon China of Stoke-on-Trent.

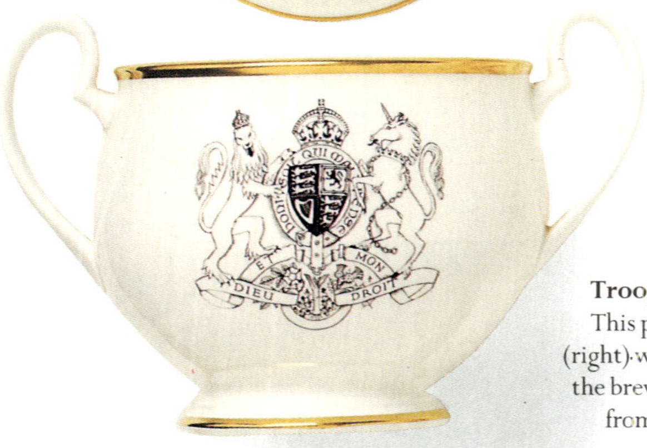

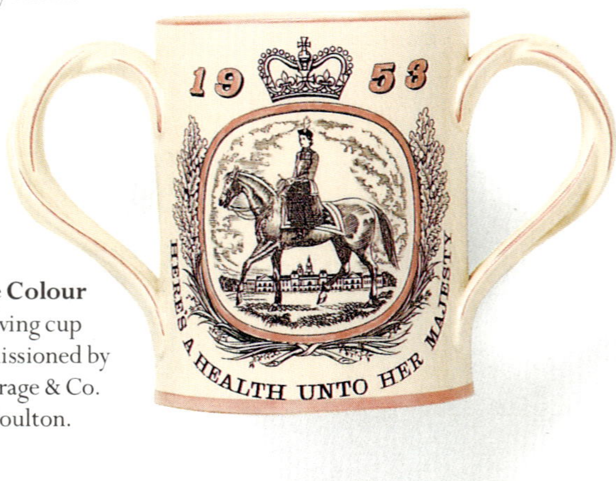

Trooping the Colour
This pottery loving cup (right) was commissioned by the brewers Courage & Co. from Royal Doulton.

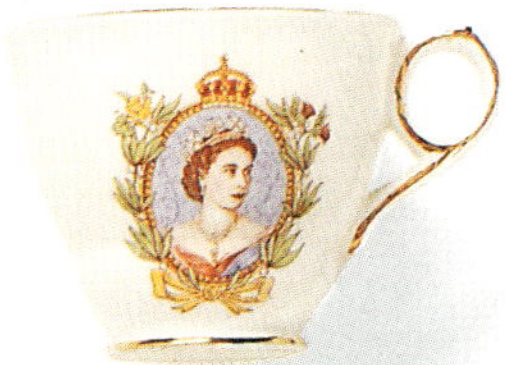

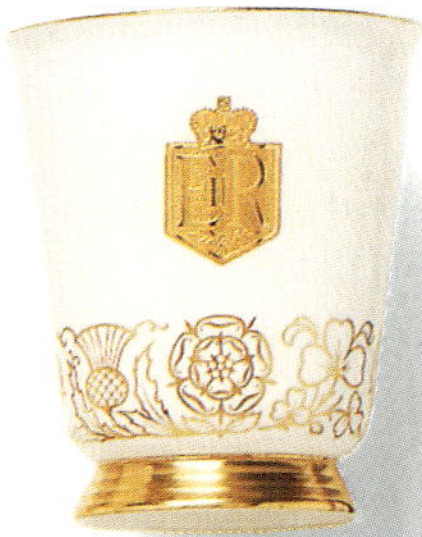

Minton
A fine porcelain beaker.

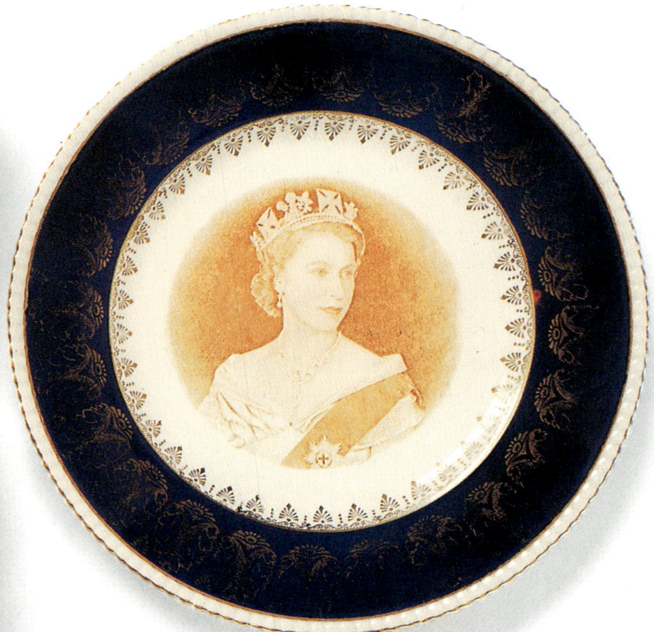

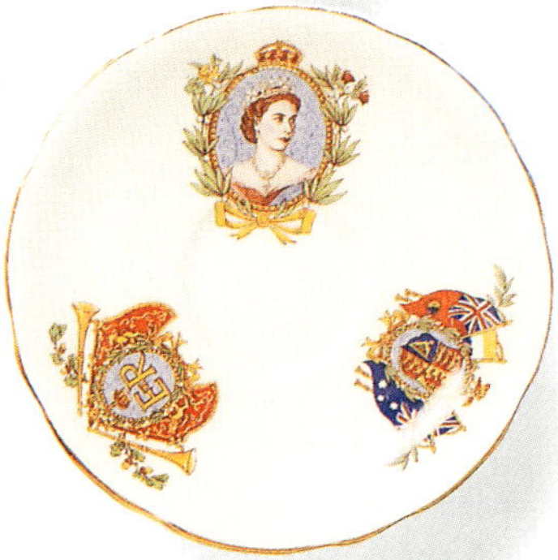

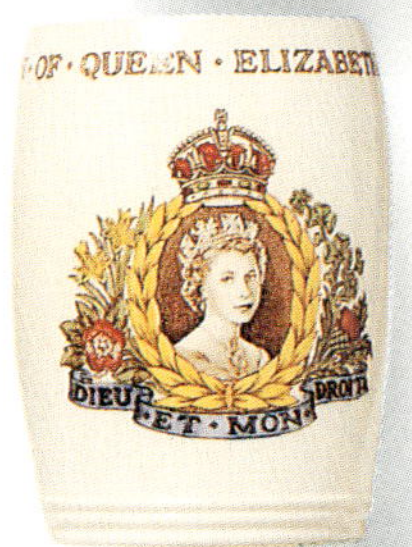

Copeland Spode
An earthenware beaker.

Royal Portrait
The photograph is by Dorothy Wilding.

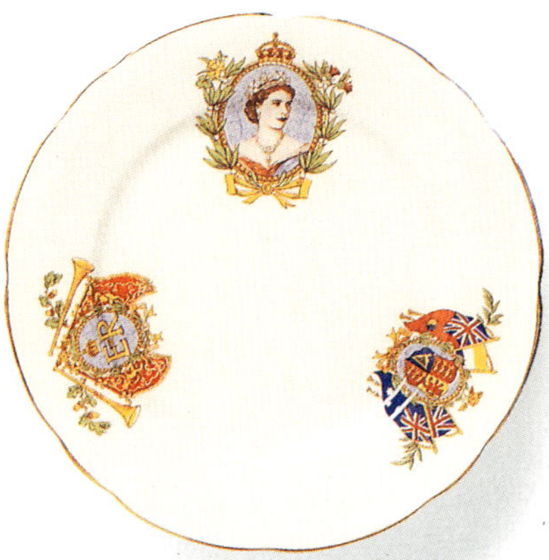

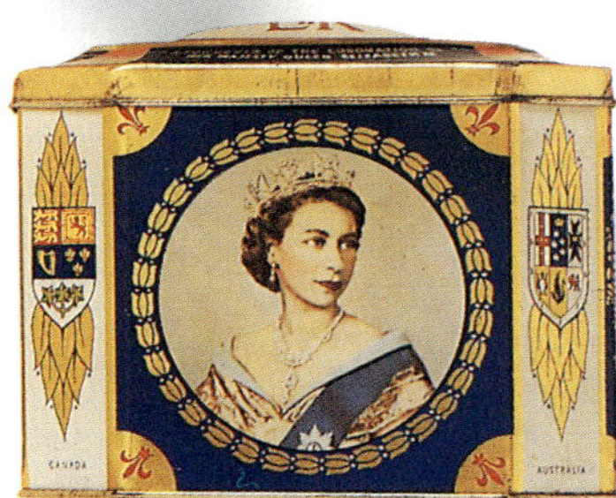

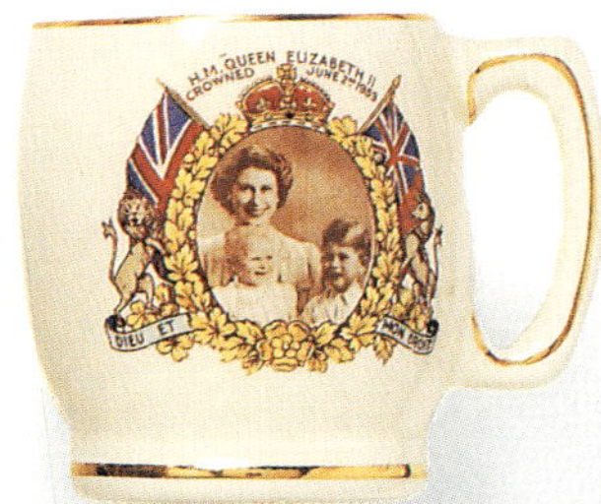

Pottery Mug
It shows the Marcus Adam portrait.

Tea Caddy
Prince Philip appears on the reverse side.

Teatime Trio
Royal Staffordshire produced this bone-china cup, saucer and plate in an unlimited edition.

Lion and Unicorn
Two pint-sized mugs by Wedgwood.

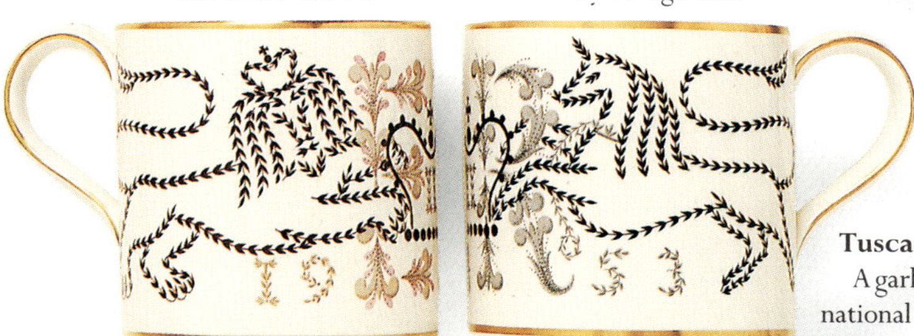

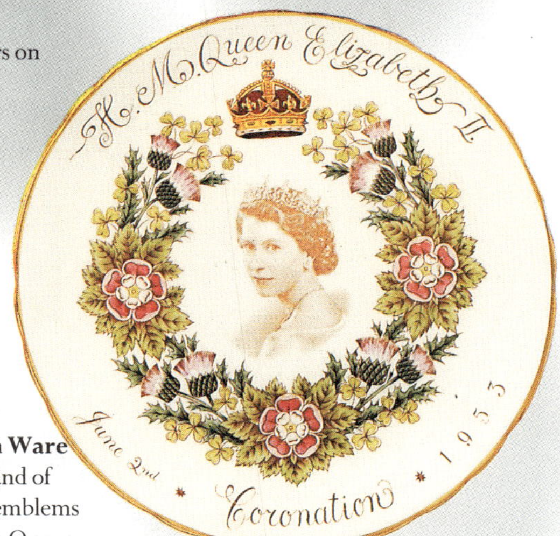

Tuscan Ware
A garland of national emblems frame the Queen.

Most of the memorabilia associated with Queen Elizabeth II have yet to become sought after as a serious investment, although there are believed to be thousands of people building complete collections of souvenirs associated with the Queen and her family. One of the rarest items is a commemorative Minton vase marking the marriage of Princess Elizabeth to Lieutenant Philip Mountbatten (HRH The Duke of Edinburgh). Although an edition of 500 vases was originally planned, it is believed that now only two survive.

The sort of commemorative memorabilia that intrigue collectors today are not those featuring the major occasions, but those which are more offbeat, such as the mug by the Staffordshire pottery Caverswall, that commemorated not the marriage but the betrothal of the Prince of Wales and Lady Diana Spencer.

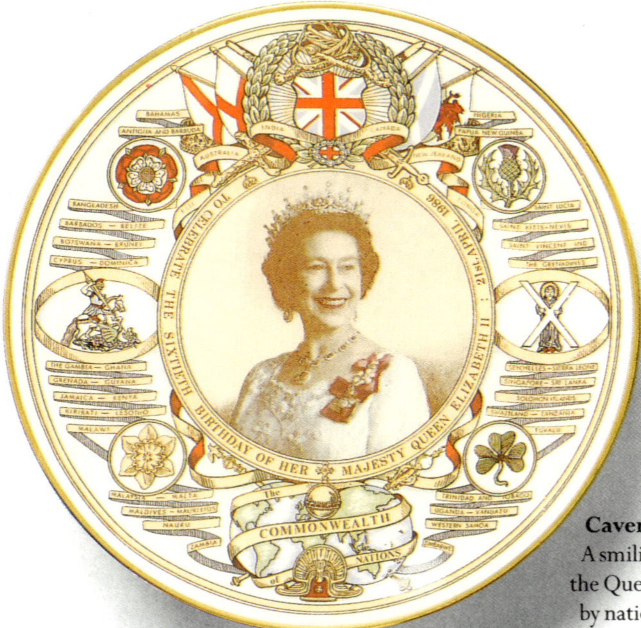

Caverswall China
A smiling portrait of the Queen surrounded by national emblems.

Quality Street
A commemorative Silver Jubilee toffee tin, made by Mackintosh.

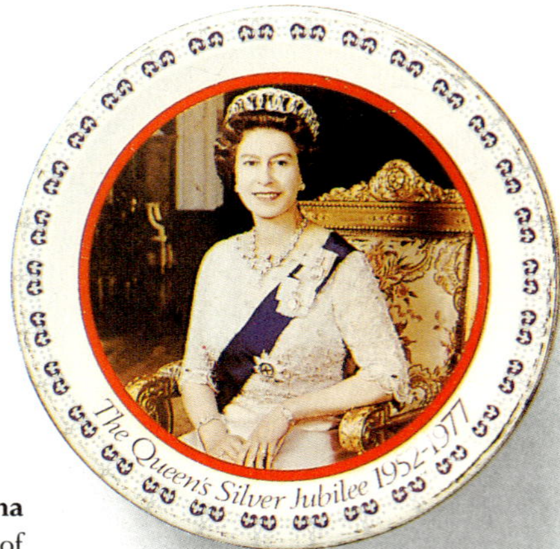

Walking Mug
An earthenware mug by Carlton.

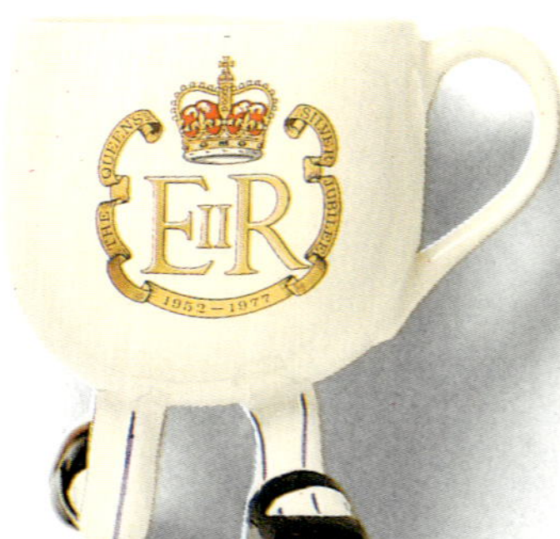

Wedgwood
A pint-sized earthenware mug designed by Richard Guyatt.

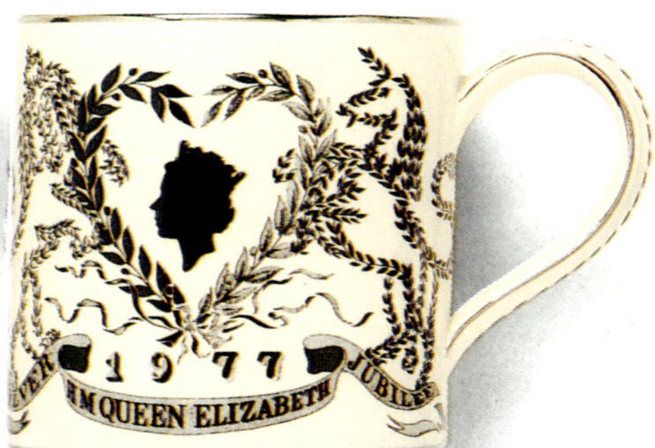

Sutherland
A bone china mug, made for the Peter Jones collection, Wakefield.

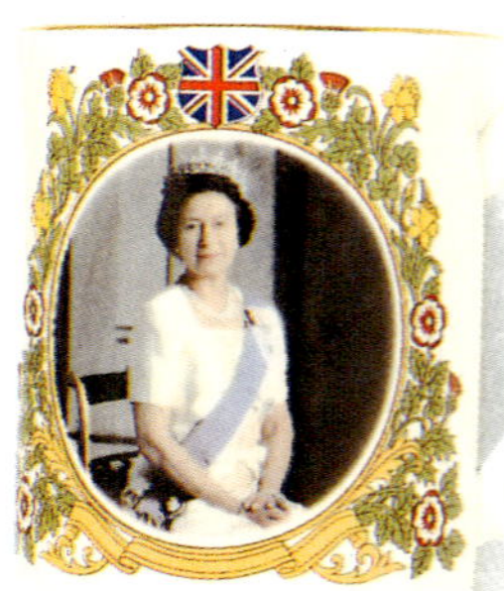

Crown Staffordshire
Two pieces marking the Silver Jubilee. The plate (far right) is from a limited edition of 10,000.

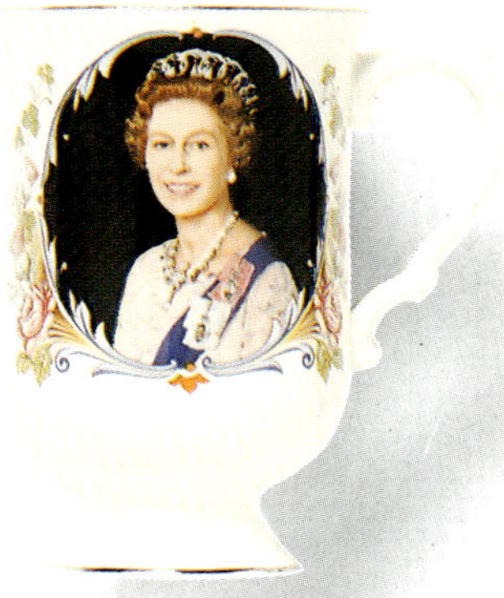

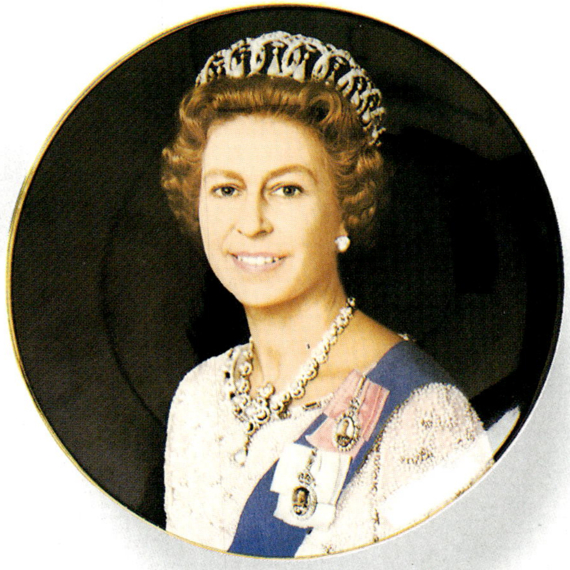

Wedgwood
This ten-inch plate is number 707 in a limited edition of 1,000.

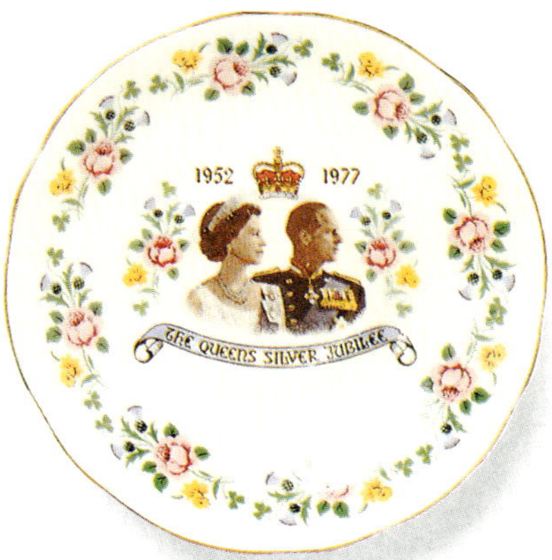

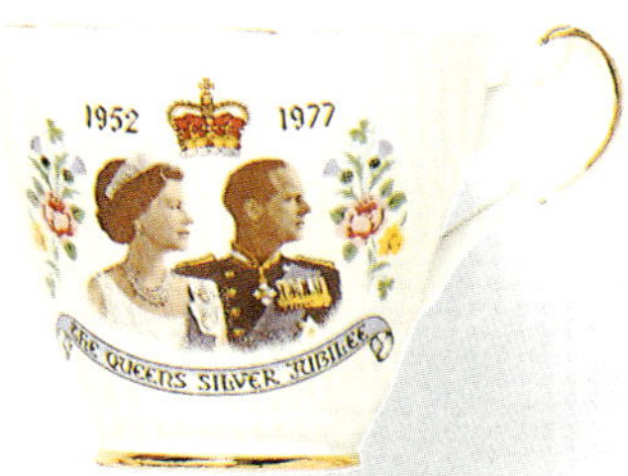

Queen and Consort
A decorative bone china cup and saucer.

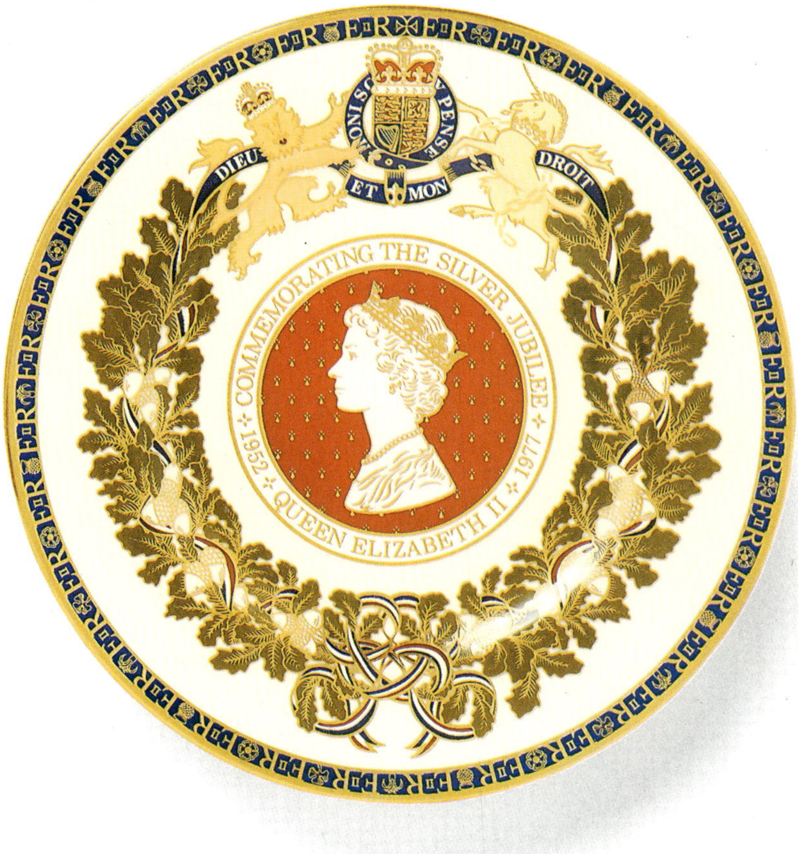

The Royal Collection

The Royal Collection, held in trust for the nation by Queen Elizabeth II, is the largest private holding of works of art in the world. Bald statistics cannot fail to impress. For where the National Gallery in London has just over 2,000 paintings, the Royal Collection has about 7,000. In addition there are 30,000 drawings and watercolours, over 2,000 miniatures and about 500,000 prints.

Over the centuries royal collectors have displayed widely varying tastes. Among the most important collectors have been Henry VIII, Charles I, Frederick, Prince of Wales, George III, George IV, Queen Victoria and Prince Albert.

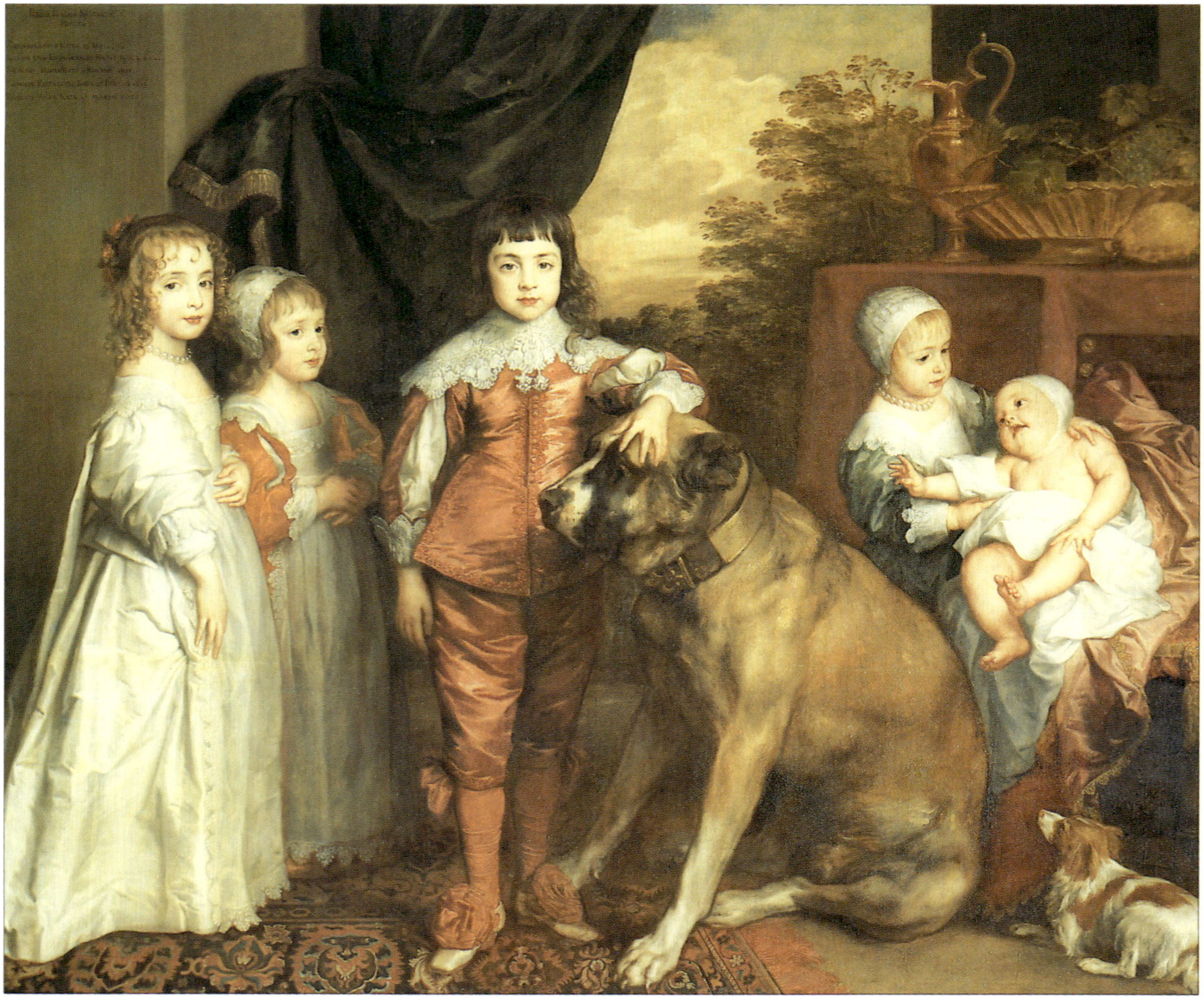

Sir Anthony Van Dyck

Van Dyck was for a time in the service of Charles I, perhaps the greatest and most ambitious British royal collector. This painting, 'The Five Eldest Children of Charles I' is one of his many famous portraits of the Royal Family.

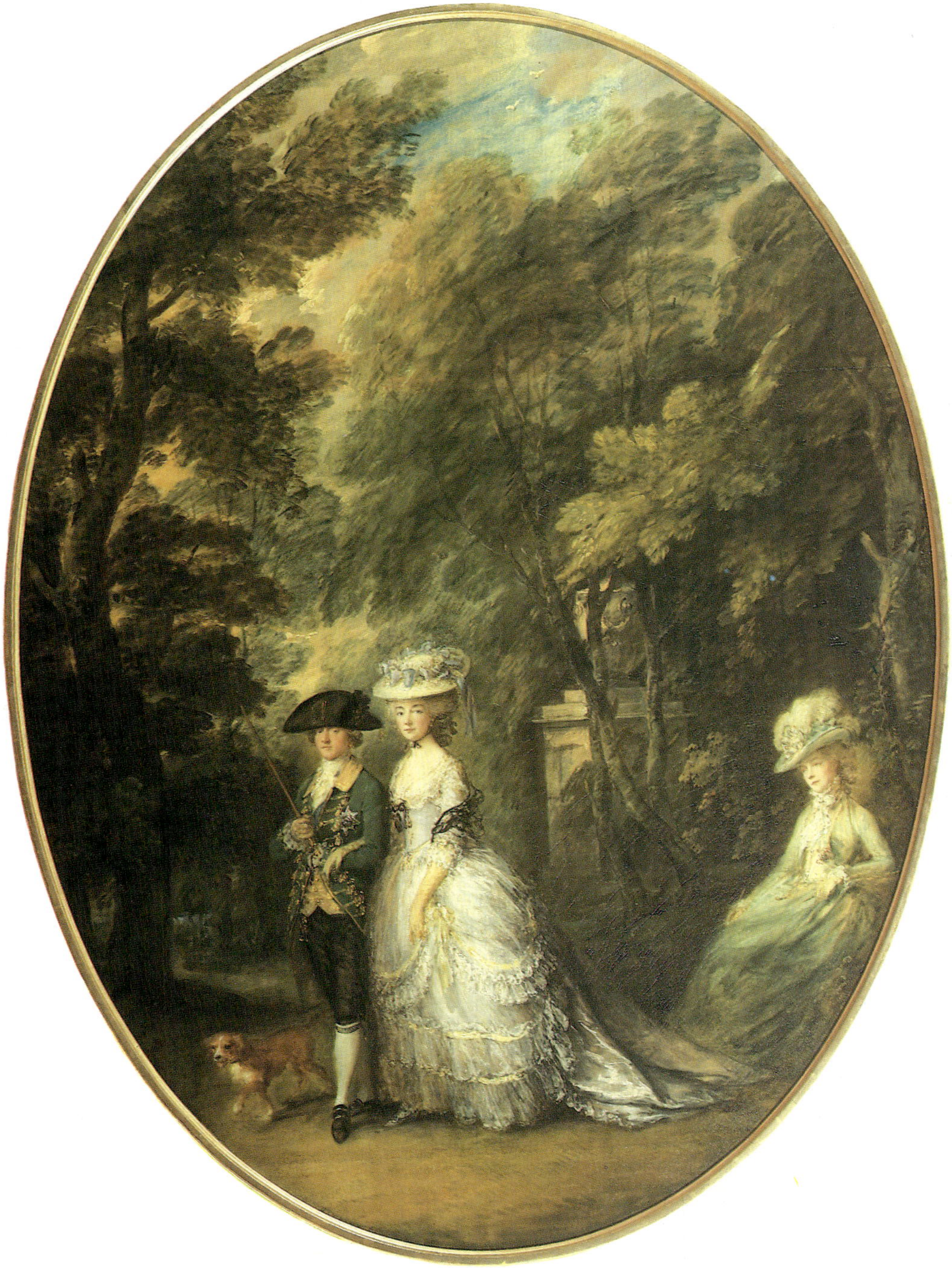

Thomas Gainsborough
The paintings by Thomas Gainsborough in the Royal Collection are unsurpassed. Shown here is his portrait of 'Henry, Duke of Cumberland, with the Duchess of Cumberland and Lady Elizabeth Lutterell'.

The Royal Collection has outstanding holdings of Dutch and English paintings, which include works by Rembrandt, Cuyp, Van Dyck, Reynolds and Gainsborough. The collection of Leonardo da Vinci and Holbein drawings is unparalleled, while the collections of Sèvres porcelain and French furniture are of the finest quality.

The Royal Collection is also rich in animal paintings. In addition to a number of fine paintings by Stubbs, it has many by Landseer, whose work was a great favourite of Queen Victoria. The Queen has continued this tradition by commissioning several paintings of her favourite animals, including 'The Queen's nine Corgis and Dorgis' by Susan Crawford.

While the Collection was of course formed to furnish and adorn the royal palaces and residences, its treasures have often been placed on exhibition in the past, and during the Queen's stewardship more works of art have been made accessible to the public in this way than in any previous reign. In 1962 the Queen opened the Queen's Gallery at Buckingham Palace in which twenty-six major exhibitions of art drawn from the Collection have been held. In addition there is the Master Drawings Gallery at Windsor Castle, which opened in 1966.

Several important travelling exhibitions have been organized and among the most imaginative was the Queen's 1977 Jubilee exhibition in Australia. The paintings and other works of art were mounted on a train and taken all over Australia by rail.

George Stubbs
The British passion for animals is reflected in the popularity of animal painters. This painting (below) by Stubbs is of 'Laetitia, Lady Lade'.

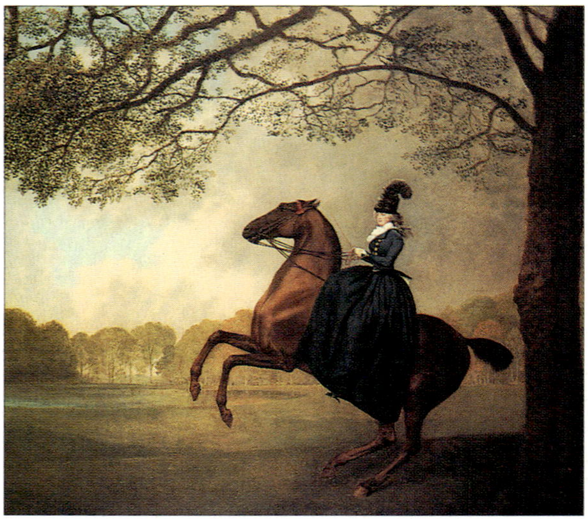

Sir Edwin Landseer
Landseer is here represented by his painting (right) of Queen Victoria's favourite pets, 'Hector, Nero and Dash with the Parrot, Lory'.

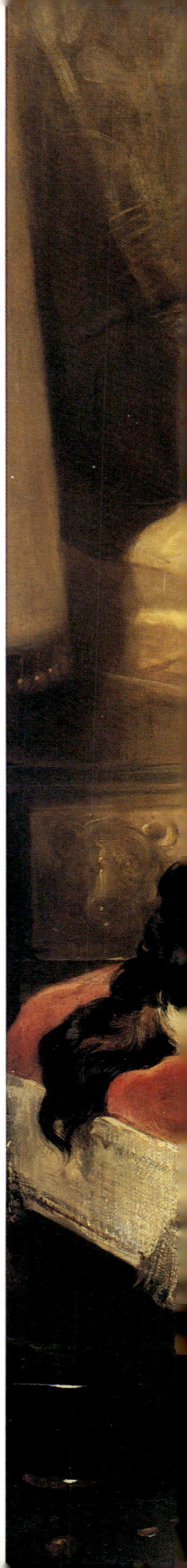

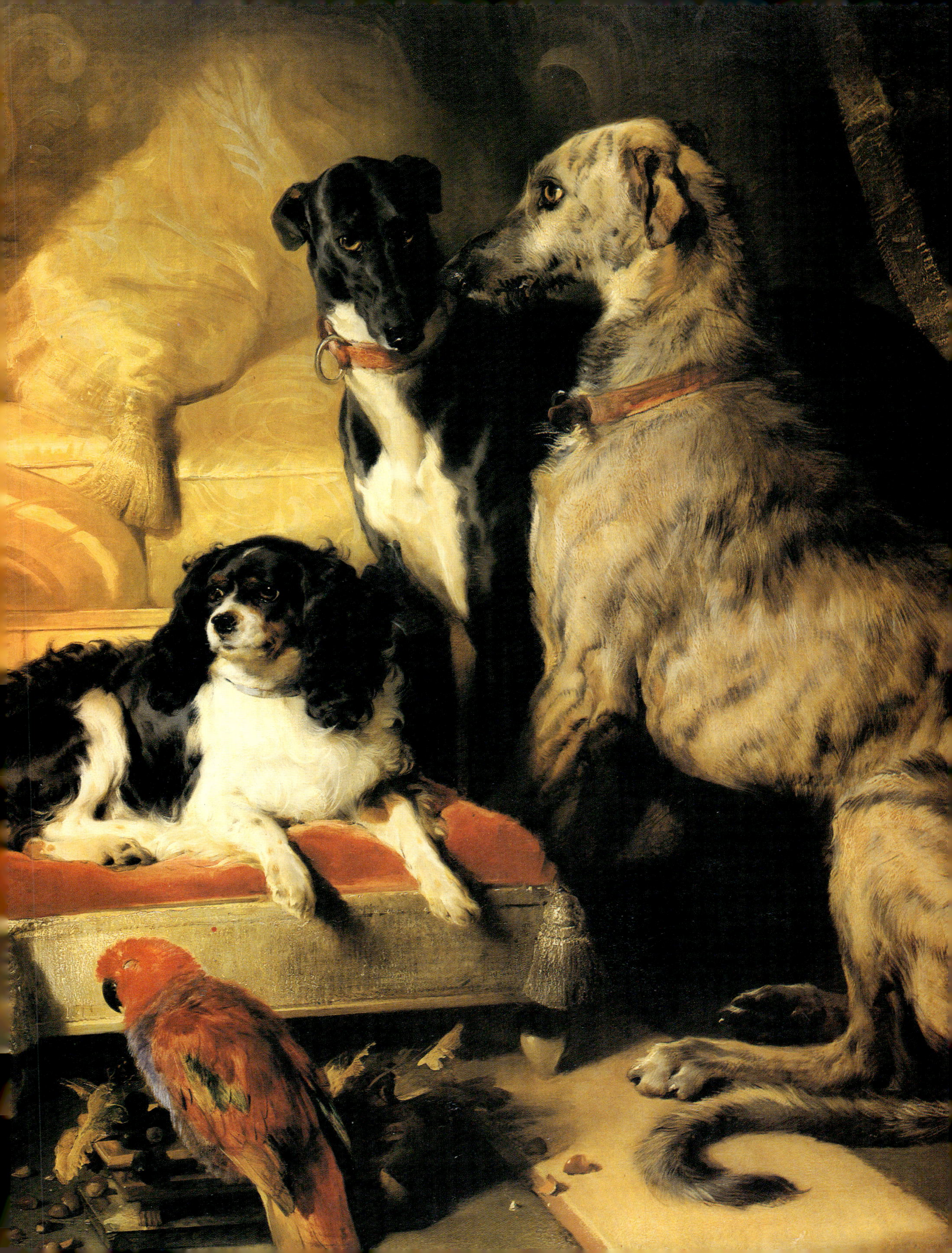

ROYAL COLLECTORS

HENRY VIII, who was the first monarch to start assembling a collection of works of art, could be described as the founder of the Royal Collection. Among the most attractive sculptures surviving from his collection is a painted terracotta bust of a boy, believed to be of Henry himself as a child. Today the collection of sculpture amounts to approximately 1,400 pieces, many of the most important having been acquired by George IV.

The collection of decorative and applied art grew substantially in the eighteenth and nineteenth centuries. George III and George IV, especially the latter, were major collectors in almost every field of applied art, with clocks being a particular interest. George III commissioned several astronomical clocks and he also commissioned timepieces from many of the leading English horologists.

His spending did not match that of George IV however, whose acquisitions include an unrivalled collection of eighteenth-century Sevrès porcelain, substantial quantities of silver gilt and both French and English furniture for Windsor Castle and Buckingham Palace.

The Queen has continued the tradition of acquiring decorative objects, especially pieces which are historically linked with her forebears.

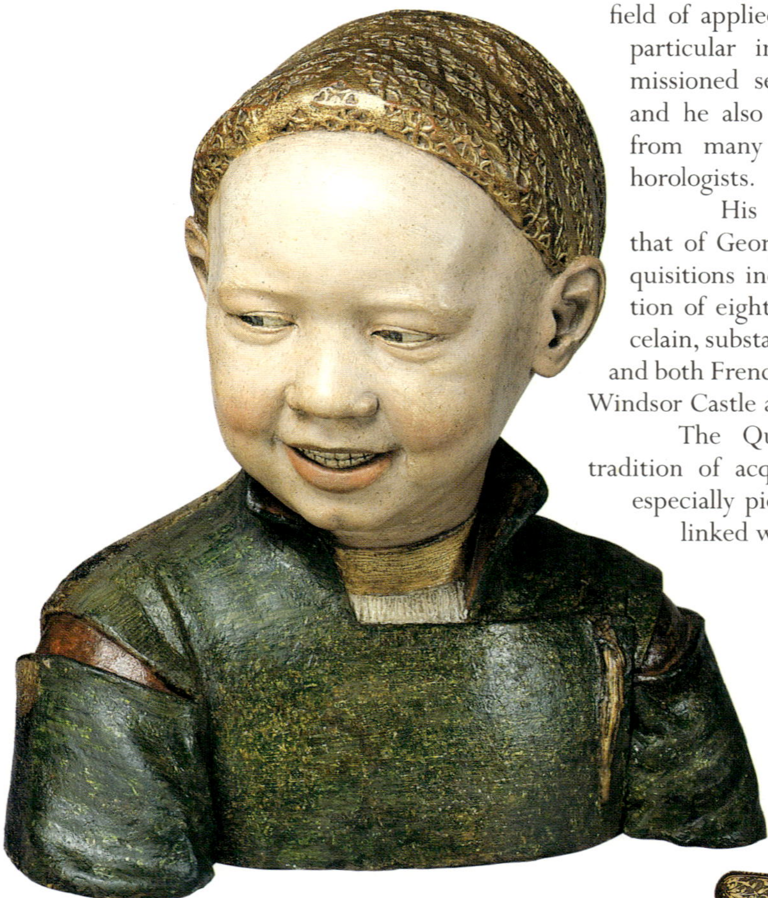

Bust of Henry VIII
Dated *circa* 1500 and attributed to Guido Mazzoni, this rare early coloured terracotta bust of Henry VIII is one of the prizes of the extensive royal sculpture collection.

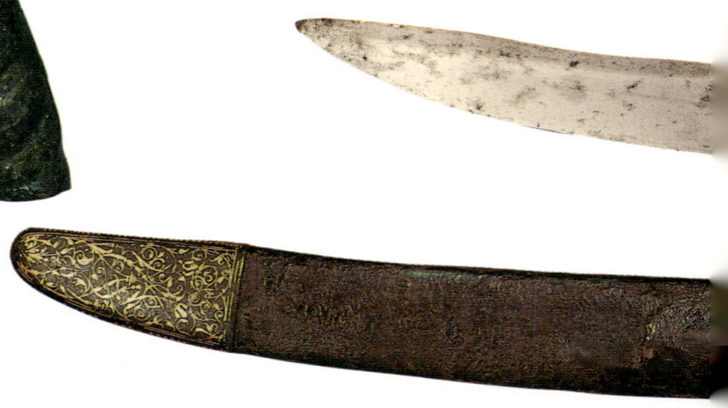

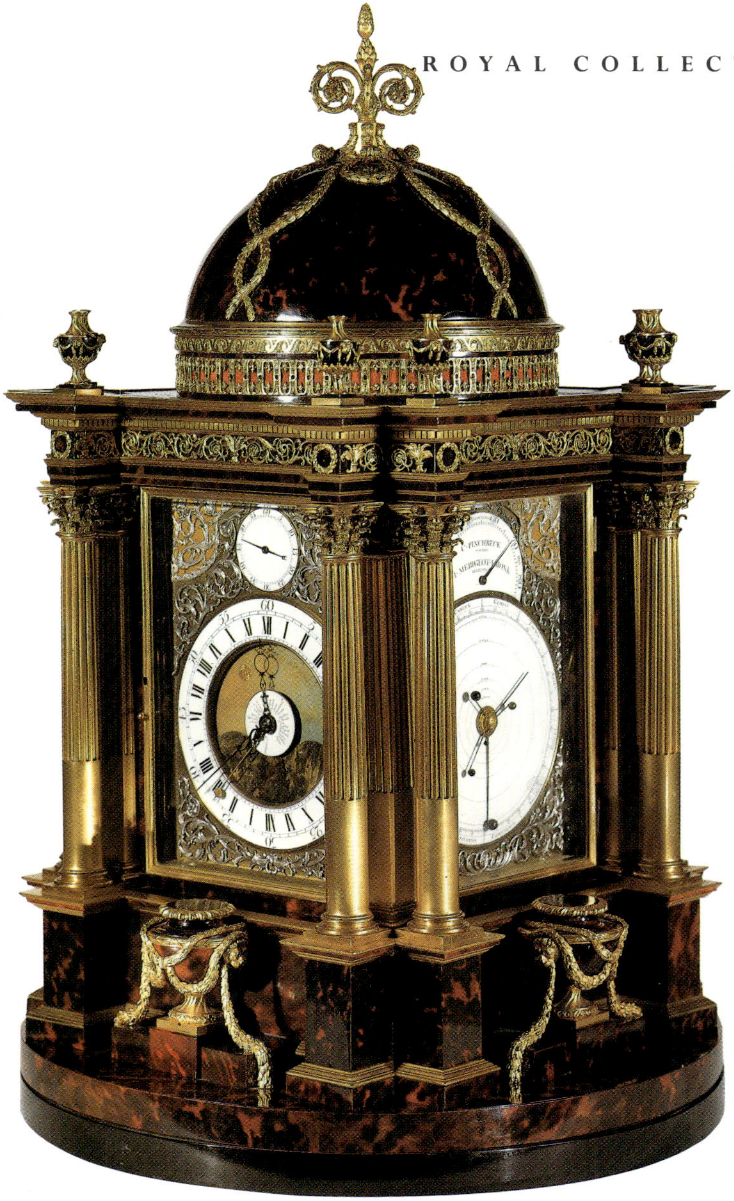

An Astronomical Clock
George III had a passion for astronomy and was an enthusiastic collector of clocks. This astronomical clock, designed and made by Christopher Pinchbeck, has a tortoiseshell and gilt bronze case designed jointly by the King and the architect Sir William Chambers.

Henry VIII's Sword
This hunting sword is thought to have been the work of Diego de Caias, a Spanish craftsman known to have been in the service of Henry VIII and Edward VI between 1542 and 1549. The scene on the blade is a representation of the siege of Boulogne by the English army under Henry VIII, in the late summer of 1544. It was acquired for the Royal Collection in 1966.

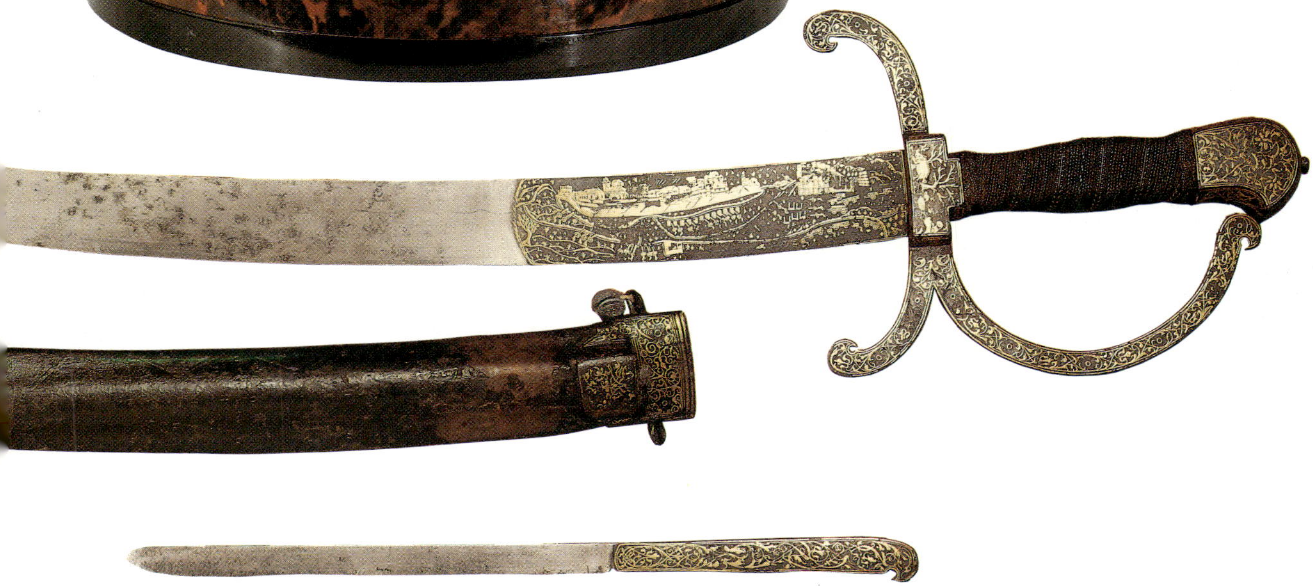

The FABERGÉ COLLECTION

PETER CARL FABERGÉ (1846-1920) was a Russian goldsmith and jeweller. His father Gustav had opened a jewellery shop in St Petersburg in 1842 and Peter, having travelled extensively in Europe, took over the family firm in 1870. With his younger brother Agathon he built a company employing five hundred designers, goldsmiths, modellers, enamellers and gem cutters, until its disbandment in 1918.

The most famous Fabergé curios are the extravagant and elaborate Easter eggs. Each egg, whose shell is encrusted with precious and semi-precious gems, opens to reveal a surprise inside – a carved stone flower, a little statue or an enamelled portrait. The workshops also made cigarette cases, picture frames, and sprays of flowers made from jewels and gold, standing in rock-crystal vases.

The collection of Fabergé owned by the Queen is one of the most important in the world. Most of the pieces were inherited from King Edward VII and Queen Alexandria, while George VI collected Fabergé cigarette cases.

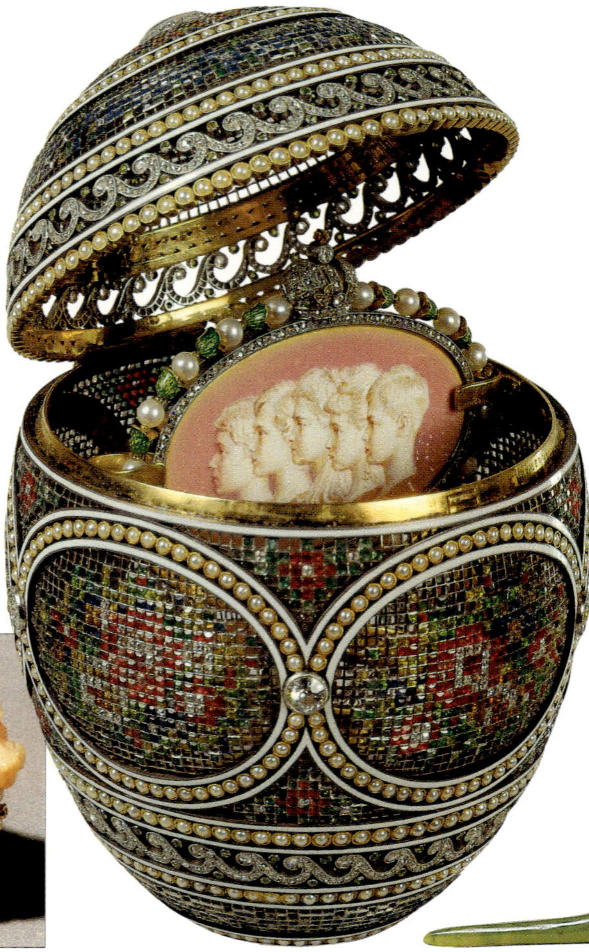

The Mosaic Egg
An Easter present for Tsarina Alexandra Feodorovna from Tsar Nicholas II in 1914, it was bought by George V and Queen Mary in 1934. This yellow gold and platinum egg contains a surprise in the form of an oval medallion with a painting of the Russian Royal children.

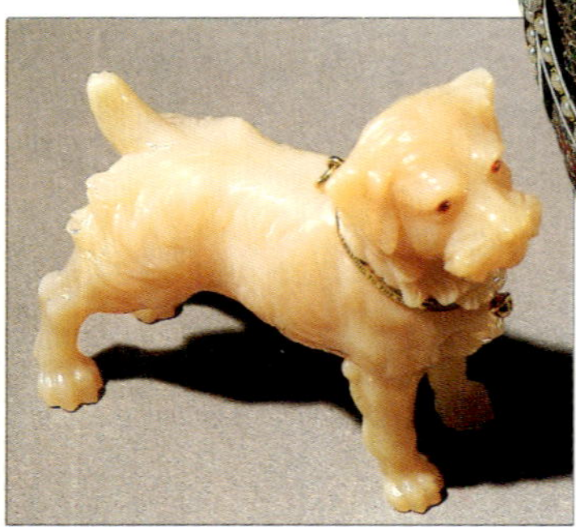

Caesar
A model in chalcedony of Edward VII's border terrier. Caesar's collar is inscribed 'I belong to the King'.

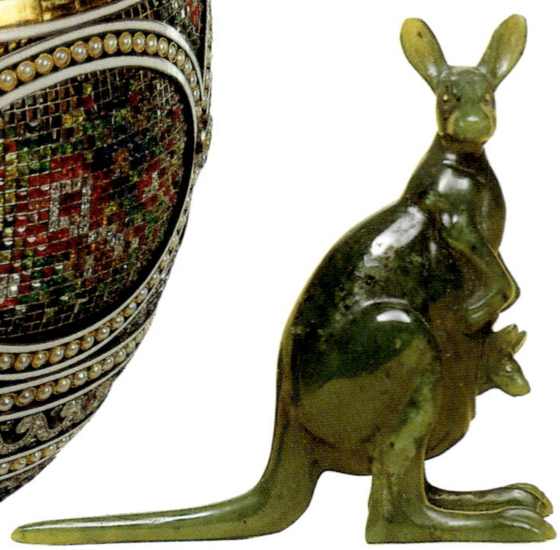

Kangaroo
One of a whole series of exotic animals that Fabergé created, it is made out of spinach jade.

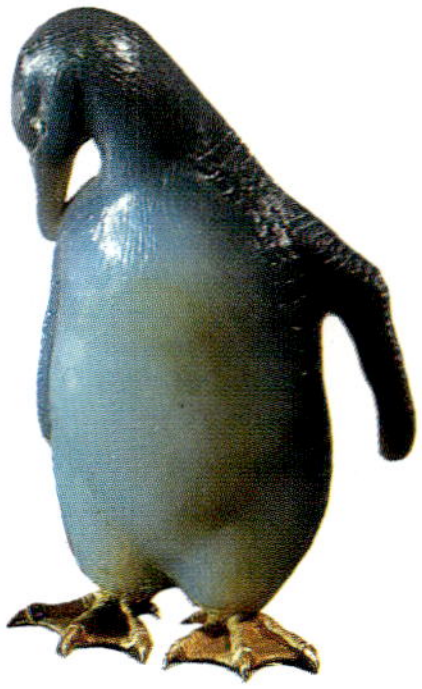

Penguin
The main body is of variegated grey chalcedony and it has rose diamond eyes and red gold feet.

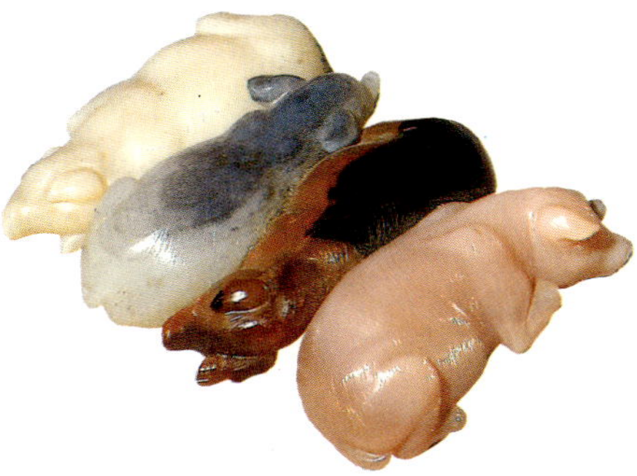

Litter of Piglets
These four sleeping piglets were crafted from different kinds of chalcedony.

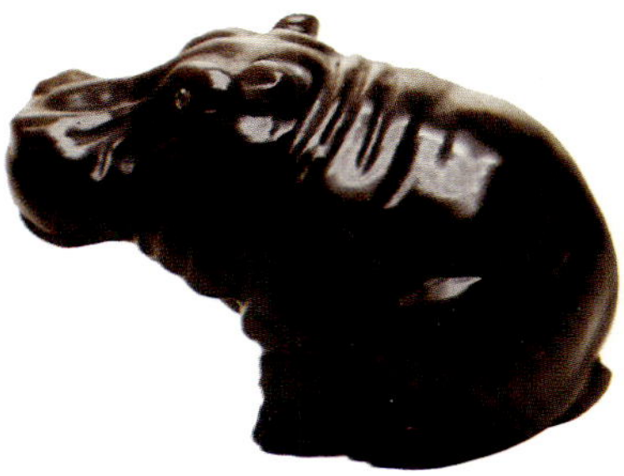

Hippopotamus
Fabergé created a number of hippopotamuses; this one is carved from obsidian, a glassy volcanic rock.

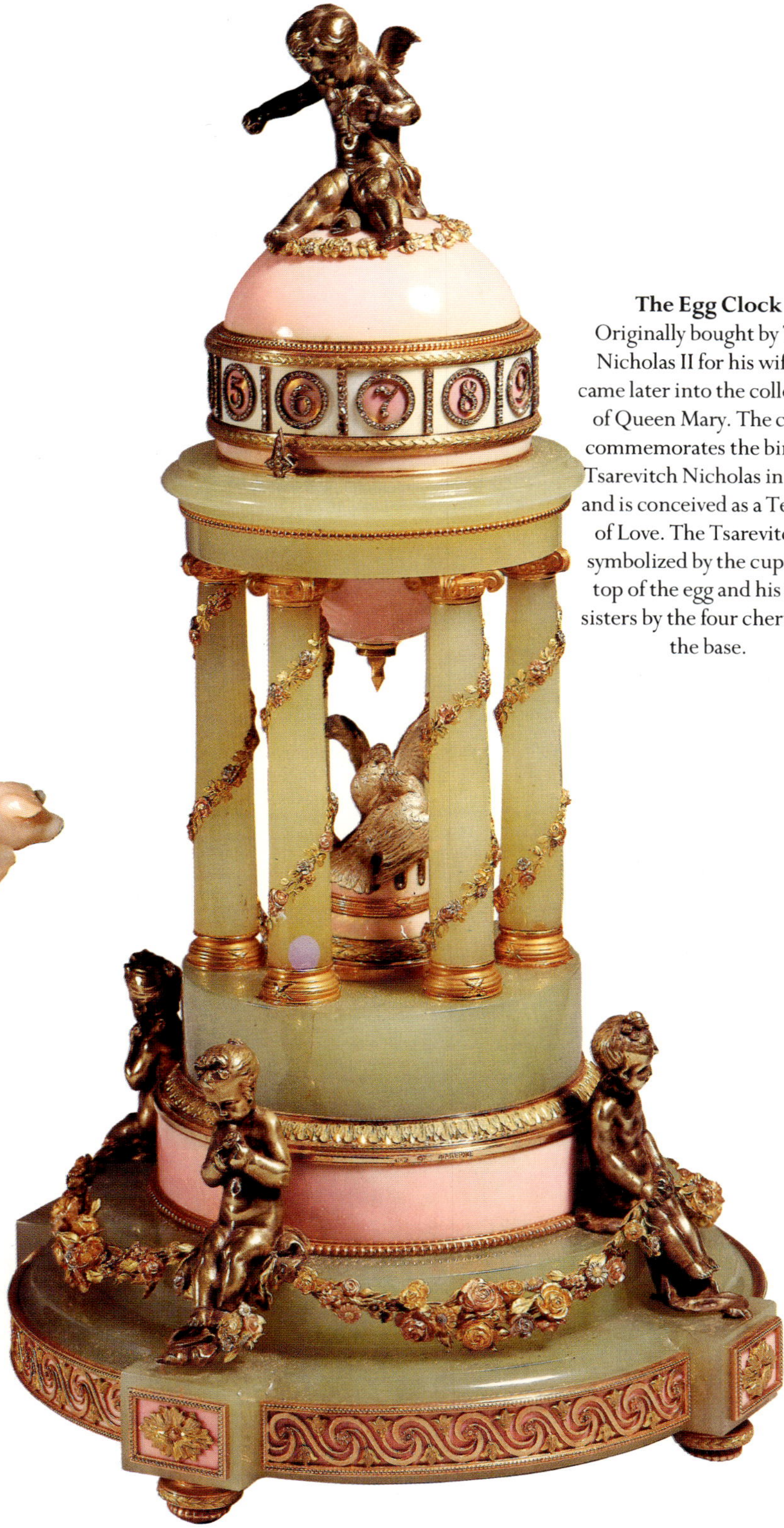

The Egg Clock
Originally bought by Tsar Nicholas II for his wife, it came later into the collection of Queen Mary. The clock commemorates the birth of Tsarevitch Nicholas in 1904 and is conceived as a Temple of Love. The Tsarevitch is symbolized by the cupid on top of the egg and his four sisters by the four cherubs at the base.

WINDSOR

WINDSOR CASTLE is a romantic collection of large buildings set in five thousand acres of park and farm land. The thousand-room royal residence began as a wooden fort in the 1070s, built for William the Conqueror and a century later it was rebuilt in stone. The royal appartments were extended in the 1360s by Edward III, founder of the Order of the Garter, who built St George's Hall for the Knights of the Garter.

In 1475 foundations were laid for one of Britain's finest late-medieval buildings – St George's Chapel. This exceptional example of Perpendicular Gothic, completed by Henry VIII, contains the tombs of ten former sovereigns, including the late King George VI.

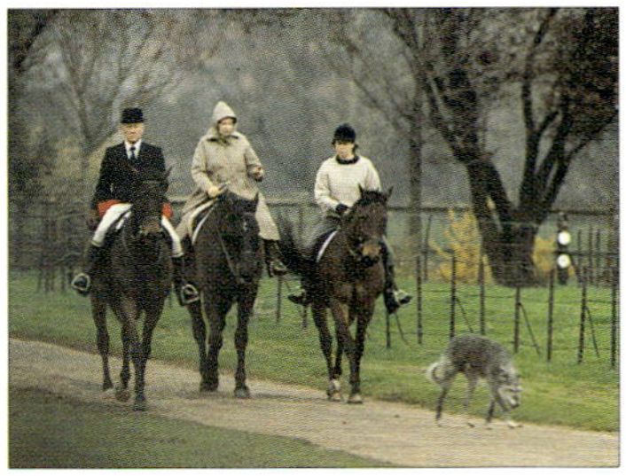

Riding at Windsor

Charles II made considerable alterations to the State Apartments and commissioned work by several eminent craftsmen including Britain's finest carver, Grinling Gibbons. He also laid out the gracious three-mile Long Walk which runs south from the castle into Windsor Great Park.

By foot or from horseback the view from the Long Walk towards the Castle is imposing. It is every tourist's idea of how a castle should be. This is no accident because in some respects the Castle has been styled into a modern conception of what a picturesque old castle should look like. This restyling occurred in the 1820s when King George

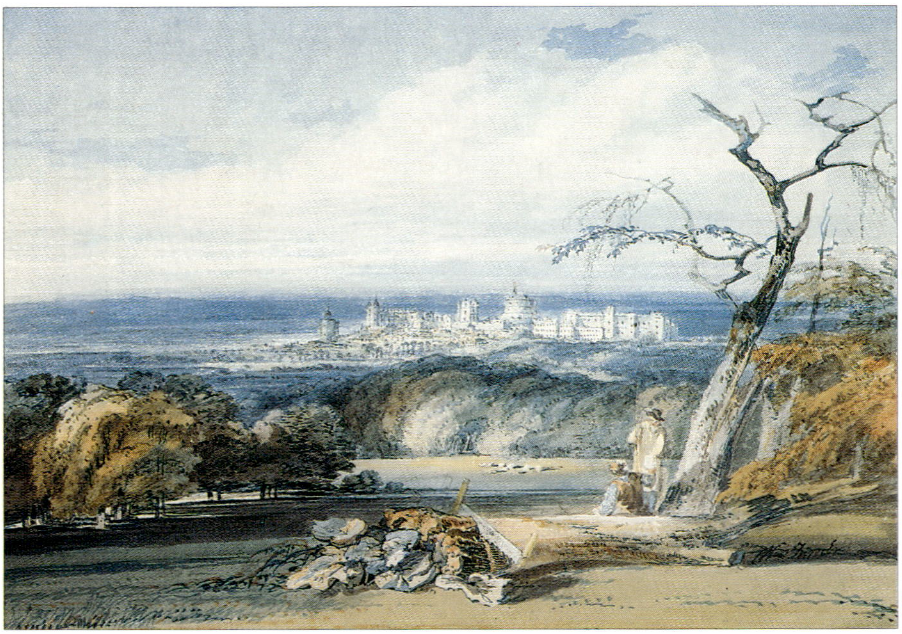

Turner's Windsor

Turner's painting, 'Windsor Castle from the Great Park', was acquired by the Queen in 1987. It is the first Turner to belong to the Royal Collection.

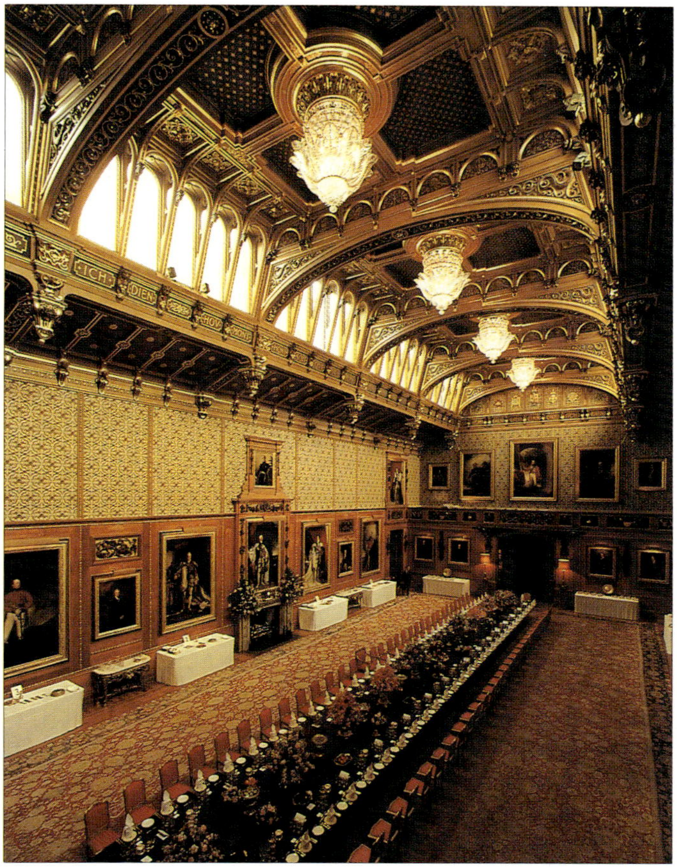

Waterloo Chamber
In this room hangs the famous series of Sir Thomas Lawrence portraits of all those who played a prominent part in the defeat of Napoleon.

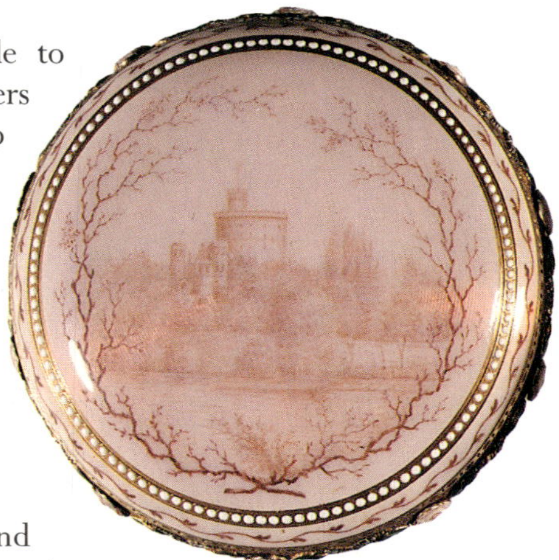

Fabergé's Windsor
This bonbonnière is one of a pair, the other depicting Balmoral.

IV commissioned the architect Sir Jeffry Wyatville to remodel the buildings with Gothic crenellations, towers and turrets. An open courtyard was covered over to form the Waterloo Chamber (in commemoration of the defeat of Napoleon at the battle of Waterloo), which is now used to host receptions and other formal occasions. The old fourteenth-century St George's Hall, the largest room in the Castle, was also altered and extended at this time. Today it is used by the Queen for state banquets.

Like her predecessors the Queen has made some changes. In the 1960s she commissioned Sir Hugh Casson to refurbish some of her private rooms and to redesign and redecorate the Royal Family's Private Chapel.

Today Windsor is in frequent use by the Queen, who spends her weekends there, as well as Easter and Royal Ascot week. Her private apartments have been described as 'country house with an emphasis upon comfort rather than opulence'. The public has access to the State Apartments, St George's Chapel and several other parts of the Castle and its grounds.

SANDRINGHAM

SANDRINGHAM, in the north of Norfolk, is perhaps the least regal-looking of the large royal houses and this is a part of its charm. Built in the late eighteenth century and acquired for the Prince of Wales in 1862, it was rebuilt as a Jacobean shooting lodge to house hundreds of people. To this day it retains an Edwardian atmosphere. This rambling country house was a great favourite of the Queen's father, George VI, who was born in Sandringham – and died there in 1952.

The house was larger in George VI's day. The Queen has had ninety of the four hundred rooms demolished because the house was becoming uneconomic. Indeed Sandringham is a good example of the Queen's general policy

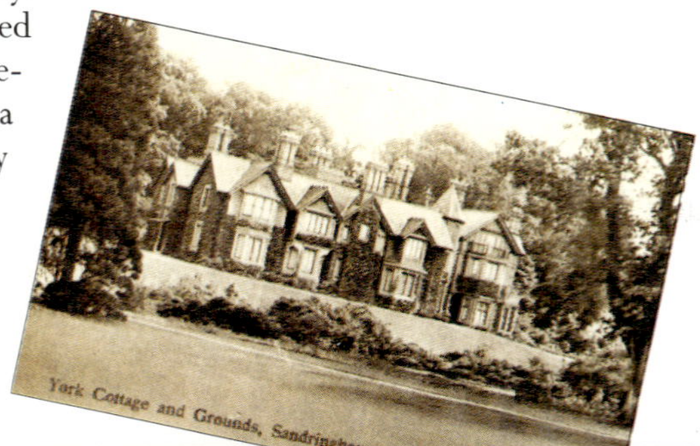

Victorian Sandringham
The Prince of Wales and party in 'A Big Shoot at Sandringham in 1867' by Thomas Jones Barker (below). York Cottage (right), in the grounds of Sandringham.

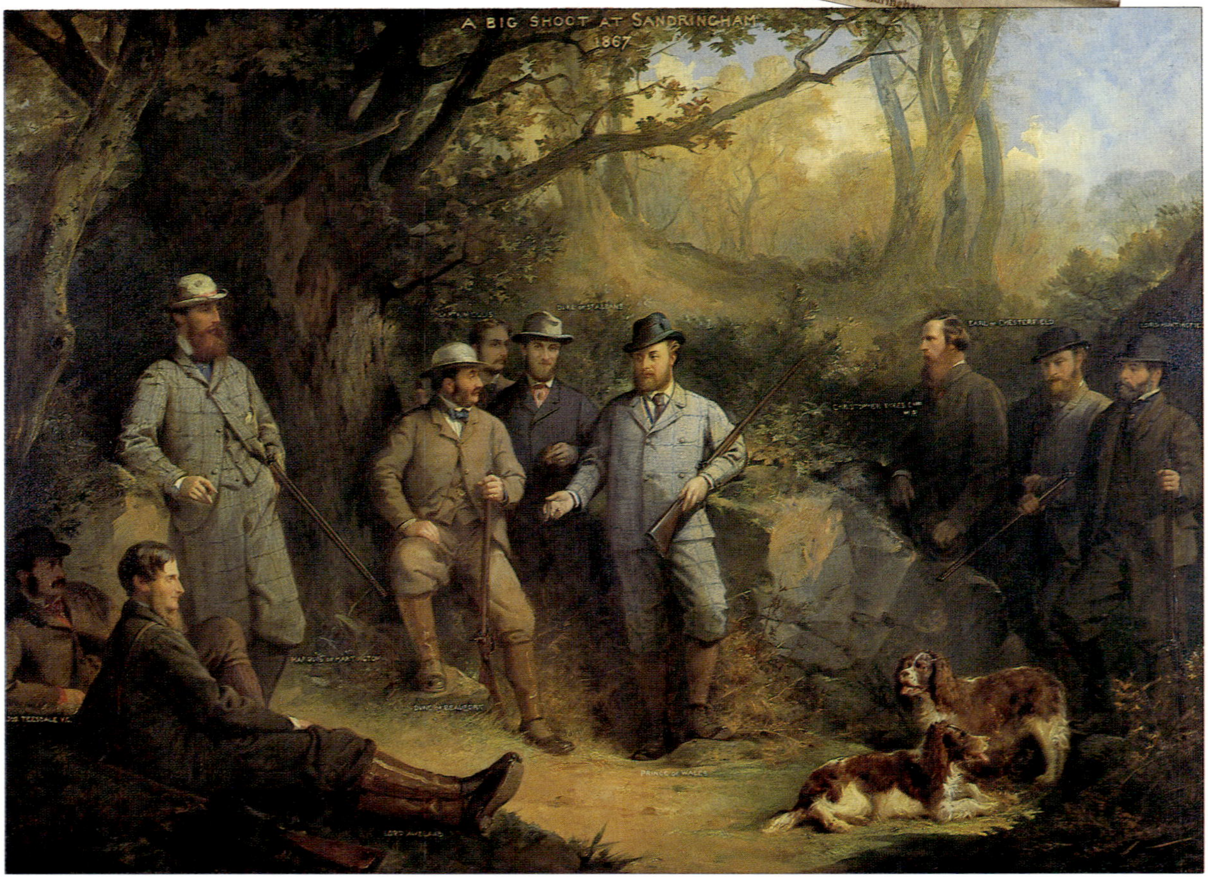

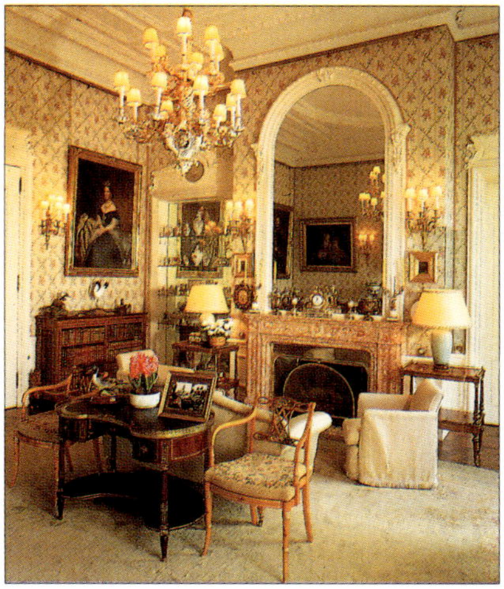

The Small Drawing Room
The portrait above the bookcase is of Queen Louise of Denmark It was painted by August Schiatt.

to make what she has inherited streamlined and efficient. She has not commissioned new houses for herself. The estate, however, has grown: originally 7,000 acres, it now covers 20,000 acres, half leased out to tenant farmers. There are extensive orchards, woodlands and a country park which is open to the public.

The estate is skilfully managed for conservation and profit: it grows and fells softwood timber on a renewable basis. Sandringham has its own sawmill and produces a wide range of timber products such as sheds and fences. In 1979-80 new glasshouses were built and these have automated equipment to regulate heating, irrigation and ventilation.

As a child the Queen spent her first Christmas at Sandringham and now, as Queen, she stays at Sandringham for Christmas and the New Year. It is a family home and it houses a number of the pictures collected by the Queen and the Duke of Edinburgh for their personal pleasure. Sandringham is also home to the royal labradors and spaniels which are bred as gun dogs for use by the Royal Family and keepers on the royal estates. The Queen takes a keen interest in the success of the kennels, which have prospered during her reign, and all the dogs are named by the Queen herself and registered at the Kennel Club with the prefix Sandringham.

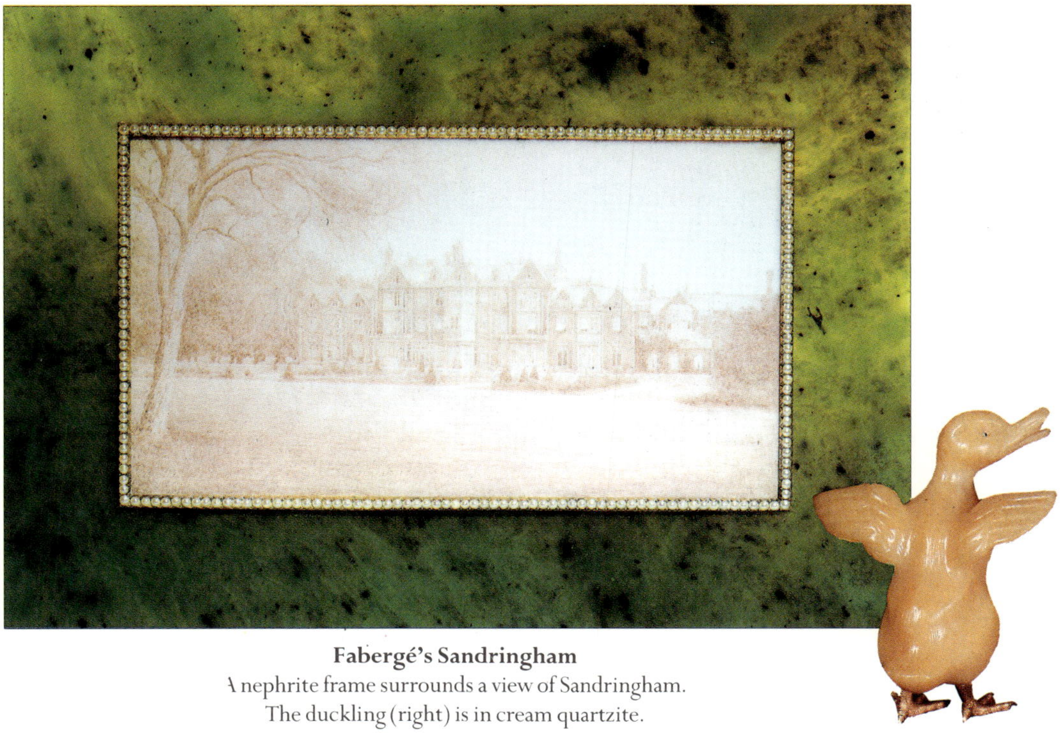

Fabergé's Sandringham
A nephrite frame surrounds a view of Sandringham. The duckling (right) is in cream quartzite.

The QUEEN'S HORSES

HORSE-RACING AND HORSE-BREEDING are two of the Queen's passions and they are both areas where her expertise is considerable. She is an expert judge of a horse, has an extensive knowledge of pedigrees and is respected as a sound reader of the form. Her particular interest is flat-racing and her horses have won four of the five English Classics – the Derby has so far eluded her.

The Queen owned her first pony in 1931 and as a child rode ponies over the moors at Balmoral; but it was at Windsor during the Second World War that she became proficient at horse care and stable management.

The first major race won by a royal horse that the Queen saw was when Hypericum won the 1000 Guineas in 1946. She inherited the Royal Studs on the death of her father in 1952 and had to wait only two years before Aureole won the Hardwicke

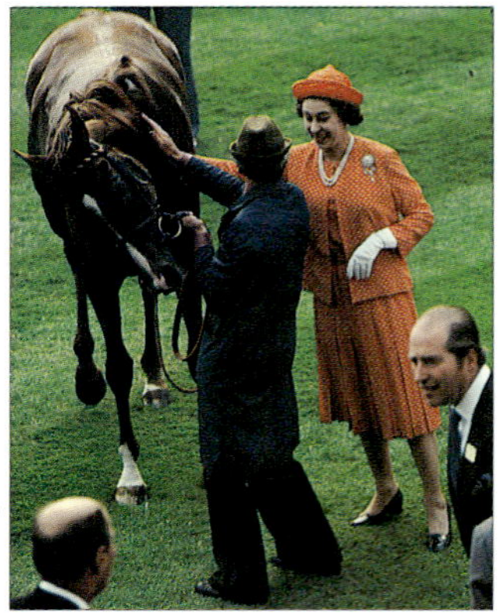

The Queen at Ascot
Like every owner, the Queen is happiest when her horses come in first.

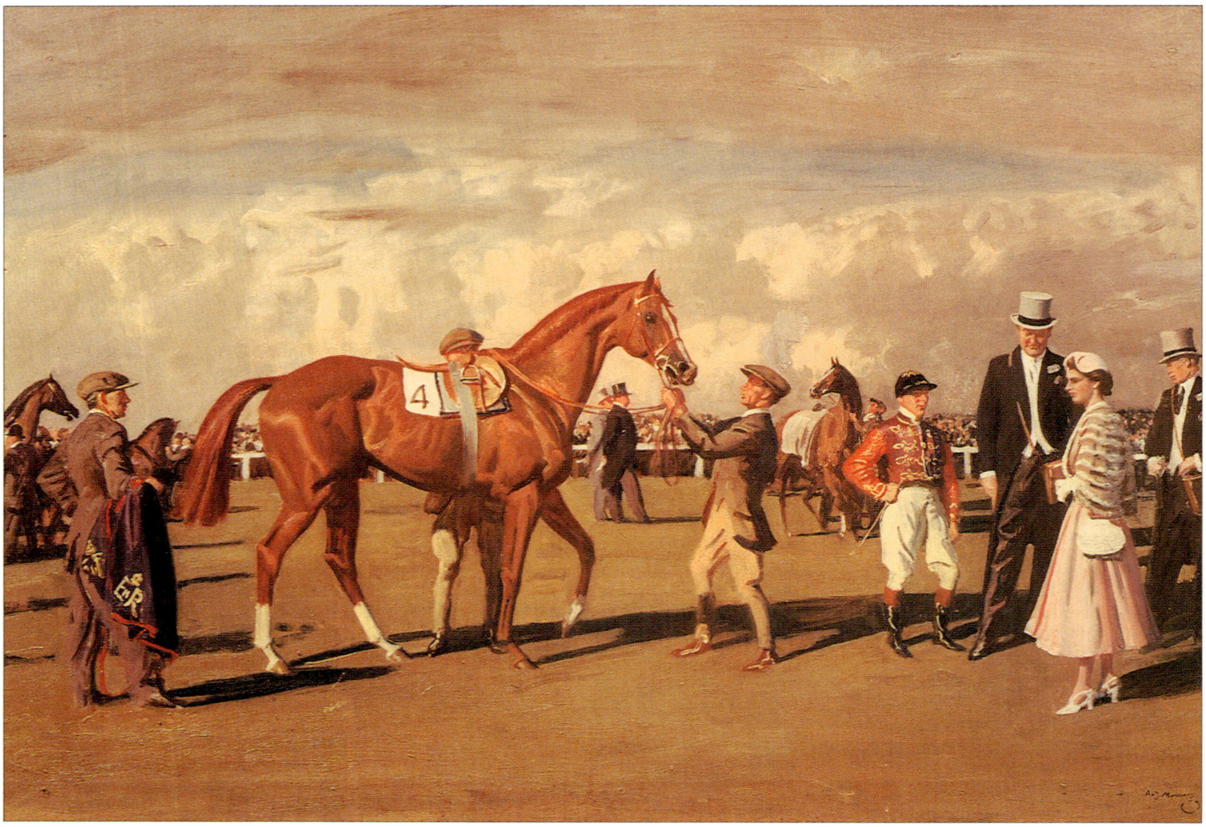

Aureole
Munnings captures the Queen with Aureole. Bred by George VI, Aureole gained his brilliant victories in the colours of the Queen. These included the King George VI and Queen Elizabeth Diamond Stakes in 1954.

Stakes at Royal Ascot, following it in the same year with the King George VI and Queen Elizabeth Diamond Stakes. Another great royal racing success from the 1950s was Almeria. In the Queen's Silver Jubilee year of 1977 the star of her stables was Dunfermline who, with a developed sense of history, won The Oaks and the St Leger.

Today the Royal Studs are divided between Sandringham and Wolferton in Norfolk and Polhampton in Berkshire. The stallions, mares and foals are based at Sandringham, while the yearlings are kept at Polhampton, the stud the Queen bought in 1972. Each year, the Queen has about twenty-five horses in training with the Earl of Huntingdon and Ian Balding.

The Queen's racing manager is the Earl of Carnarvon and although the Queen's passion for horses is one of her major pastimes, it is run as a business (although privately financed). The intention is to win races and breed good horses and many of the successes enjoyed by the Queen and her managers have been in races run in Europe and the USA.

On Horseback
The Queen is herself an accomplished equestrian. As a child she rode ponies over the moors at Balmoral.

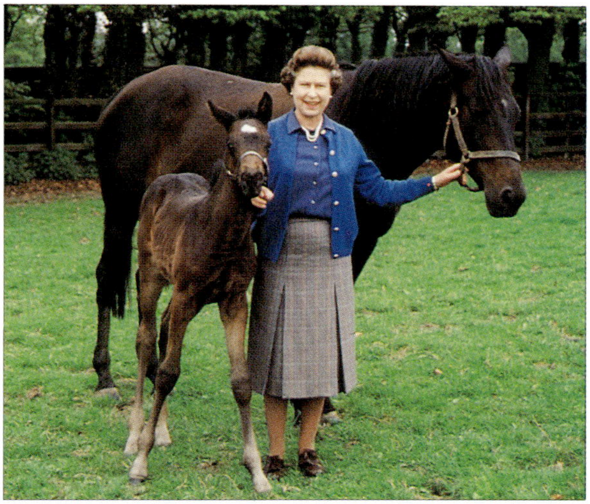

Sandringham Stud
Sandringham (left) is home to one of the three royal studs, the others being at Wolferton in Norfolk and Polhampton in Berkshire.

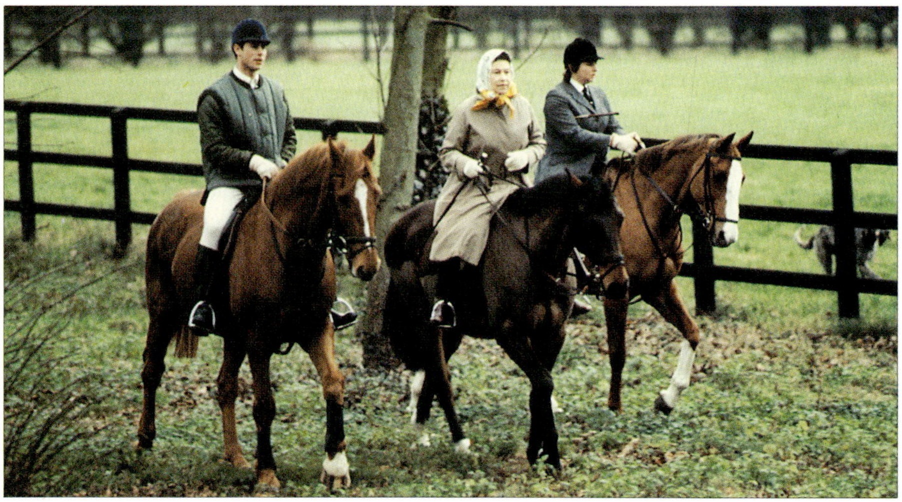

The QUEEN'S DOGS

THE QUEEN IS FAMOUS for her fondness for corgis, less so for her liking of labradors. The eleven corgis were as outraged as anyone else when, on 9 July 1982, the Queen found an intruder, Michael Fagan, in her bedroom. According to Elizabeth Longford, whilst a footman and a maid manoeuvred Fagan into a pantry, the Queen kept off 'the indignant corgis' who had arrived with the footman like a canine cavalry regiment.

There has been a corgi in the Royal Family since 1933 and the Queen received the first of her own corgis, called Susan, in 1944. Her corgis today are Susan's descendants. There is also a breed of dog special to the Queen – the royal

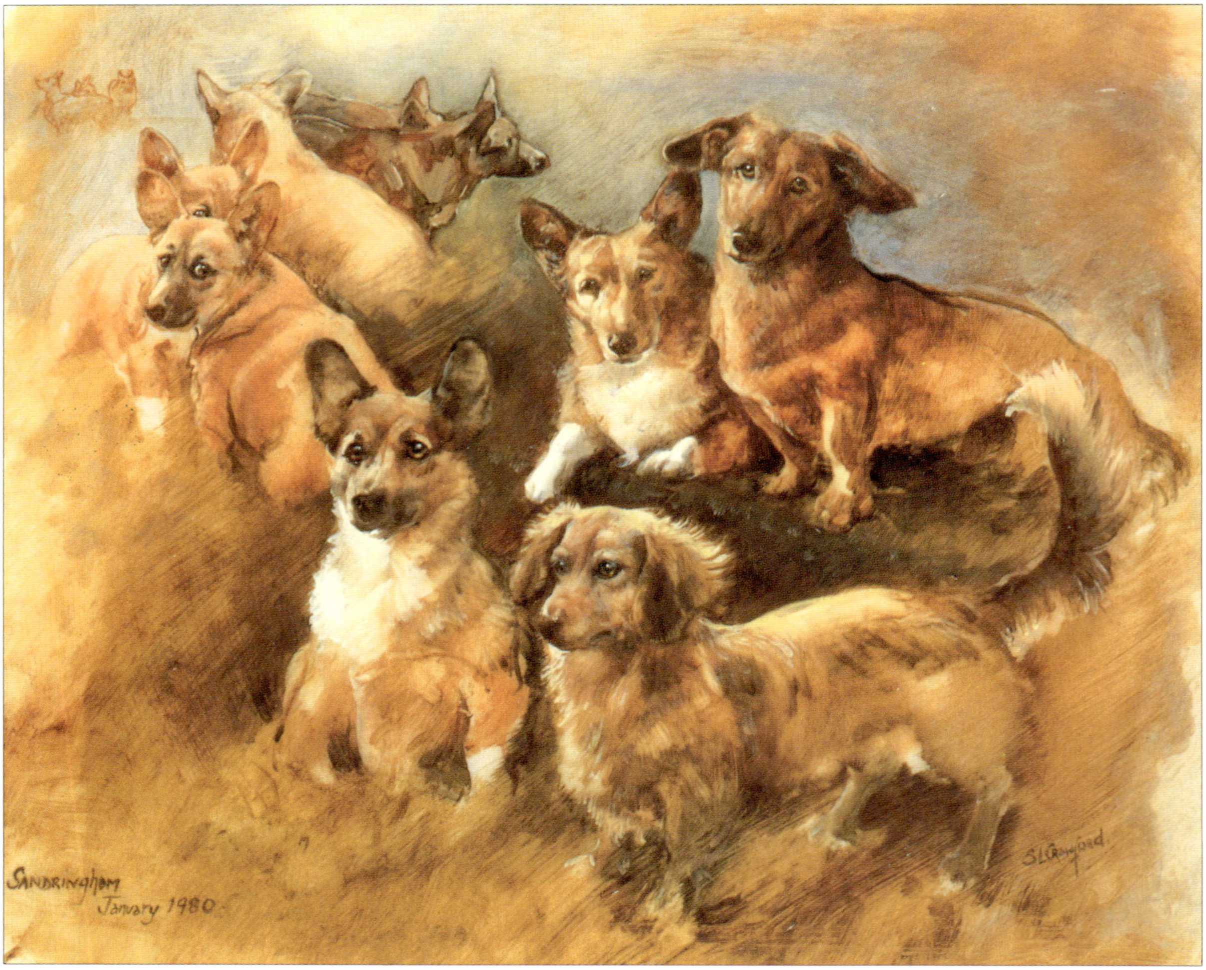

Nine Corgis and Dorgis
Like her great-great-grandmother Queen Victoria, the Queen commissions paintings of her favourite animals. Sue Crawford painted this Sandringham group in 1980.

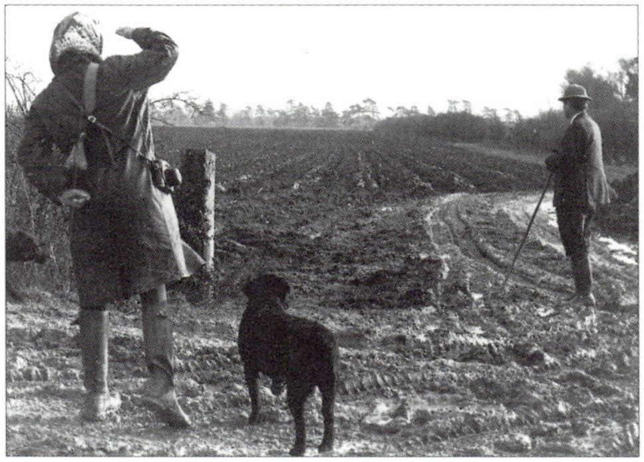

The Queen with her Labradors
The photograph was taken by Elizabeth Johnston at Sandringham in 1977.

'dorgi'; this is the consequence of a corgi mating with Princess Margaret's dachshund.

The dogs are part of the family and they travel with the Queen on internal flights with the Queen's Flight or on the Royal Train. The Queen keeps her labradors at Sandringham and four field trial champions have been trained here. Indeed it is the policy of the Sandringham kennels to train to high field trial standards as many of the dogs as are suitable.

Today there are approximately twenty dogs at the kennels, the more experienced of whom act as gundogs for the Royal Family during the shooting season, while the younger ones are still under training.

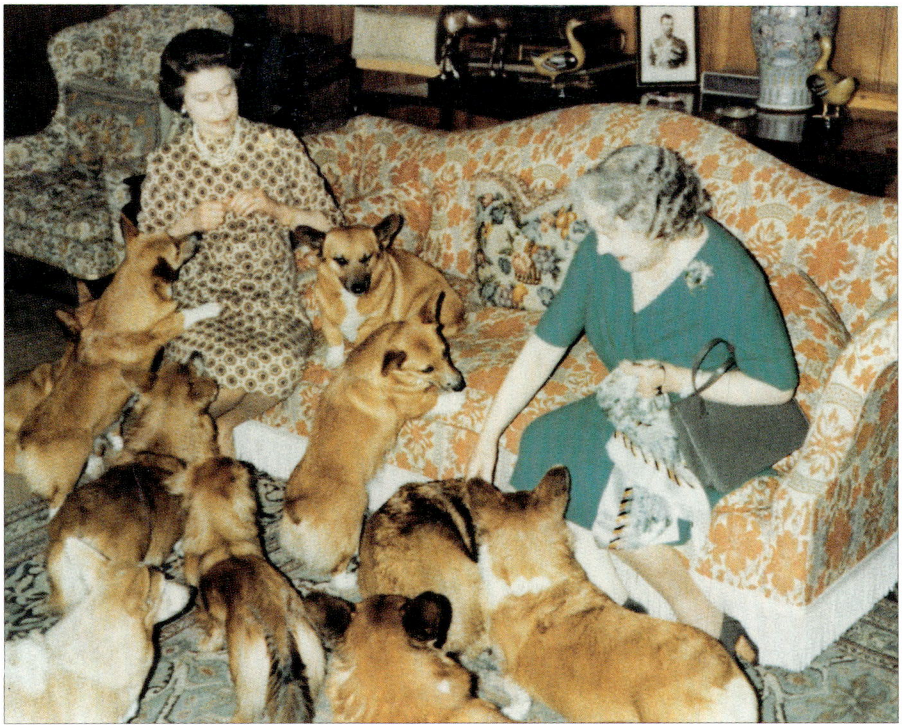

Susan's Grave
The Queen was given her first corgi, Susan, on her eighteenth birthday.

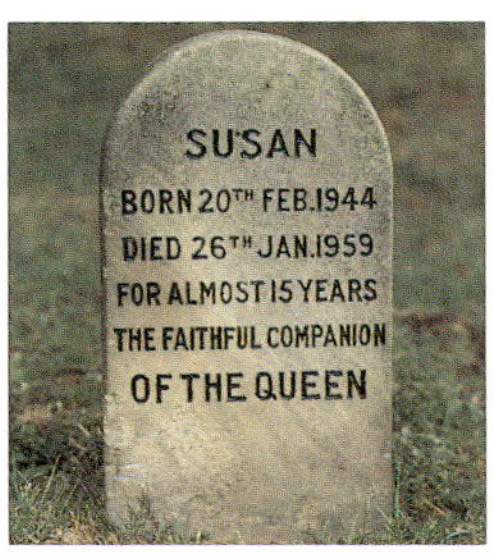

At Home
The Queen and Queen Elizabeth the Queen Mother surrounded by friends at Sandringham (above).

A CONTINUING PURPOSE

THE VISIBLE WORK OF THE QUEEN includes ceremonial occasions, banquets, state visits, tours of factories and the opening of new buildings. Even the bestowing of honours is quite a public event with friends and relatives of the newly honoured watching as the Queen bestows the medals and decorations of honour. She often manages to see 130 or more people in little over an hour – and each award is accompanied by a smile and some special words for the recipient.

But the hidden work of the Queen is as important as her ceremonial and public duties. Much of her work is directed towards keeping herself well-informed on parliamentary, ministerial, national and international affairs. Without such knowledge the Queen could not properly fulfil her duties as Head of State, and the rights that she has as a constitutional monarch – to be consulted, to encourage and to warn – would be hollow.

Wherever the Queen happens to be – at home or abroad – there is a constant stream of letters and Foreign Office and Cabinet Office papers. Her Press Secretary provides daily summaries of royal coverage in the newspapers and when Parliament is sitting, the Vice-Chamberlain of the Household provides a daily report of its proceedings. The Foreign Office conveys information to the Queen about international affairs whilst those Commonwealth countries of which the Queen is Head of State have access to the Queen's offices – they are not filtered through a British government department.

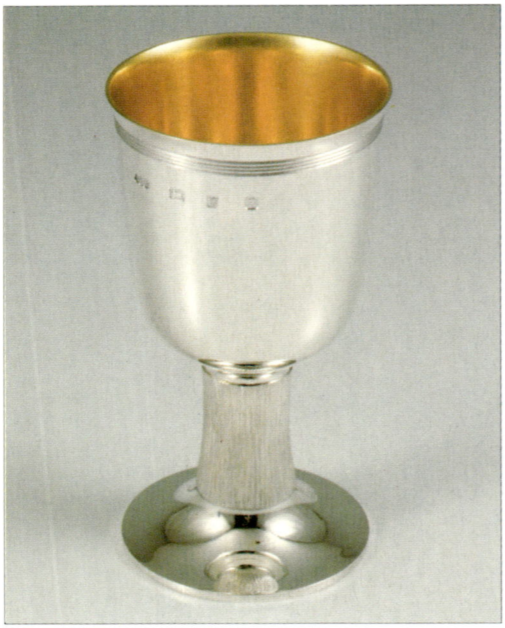

The Commonwealth Mace and Goblets

Commissioned by the Royal Anniversary Trust, the Commonwealth mace (below) is a gift to the Queen, marking the fortieth anniversary of her accession to the throne. The gold mace, designed by Gerald Benney, Goldsmith and Silversmith to the Queen, from an idea of Robin Gill, is surmounted by the Royal Coat of Arms and a cabochon ruby. The stem is a gold spiral which incorporates the fifty Commonwealth flags, painted on enamel. To accompany the mace are fifty gold-plated toasting goblets, given by and bearing the symbols of each nation of the Commonwealth.

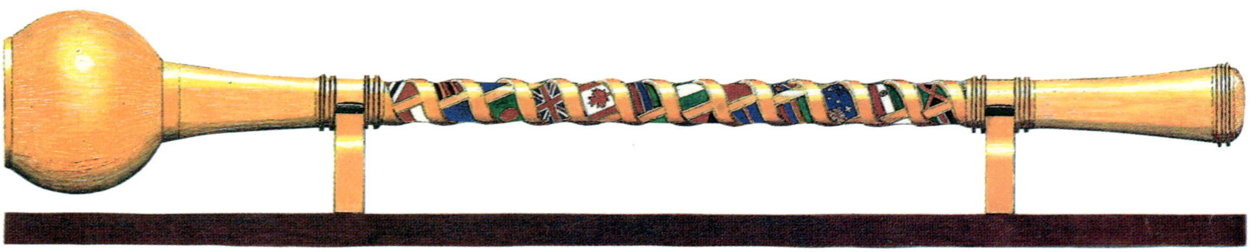

All foreign ambassadors present their credentials to the Queen when appointed; all formally take their leave of her when their period of duty is ended. All British ambassadors and High Commissioners are received by the Queen as they are formally Her Majesty's representatives abroad.

As everyone in a position to know will assert, the Queen is now the most experienced statesman in the world. In her Christmas message broadcast on 25 December 1991 she said, 'I feel the same obligation to you that I felt in 1952. With your prayers, and your help, and with the love and support of my family, I shall try to serve you in the years to come.' The work goes on.

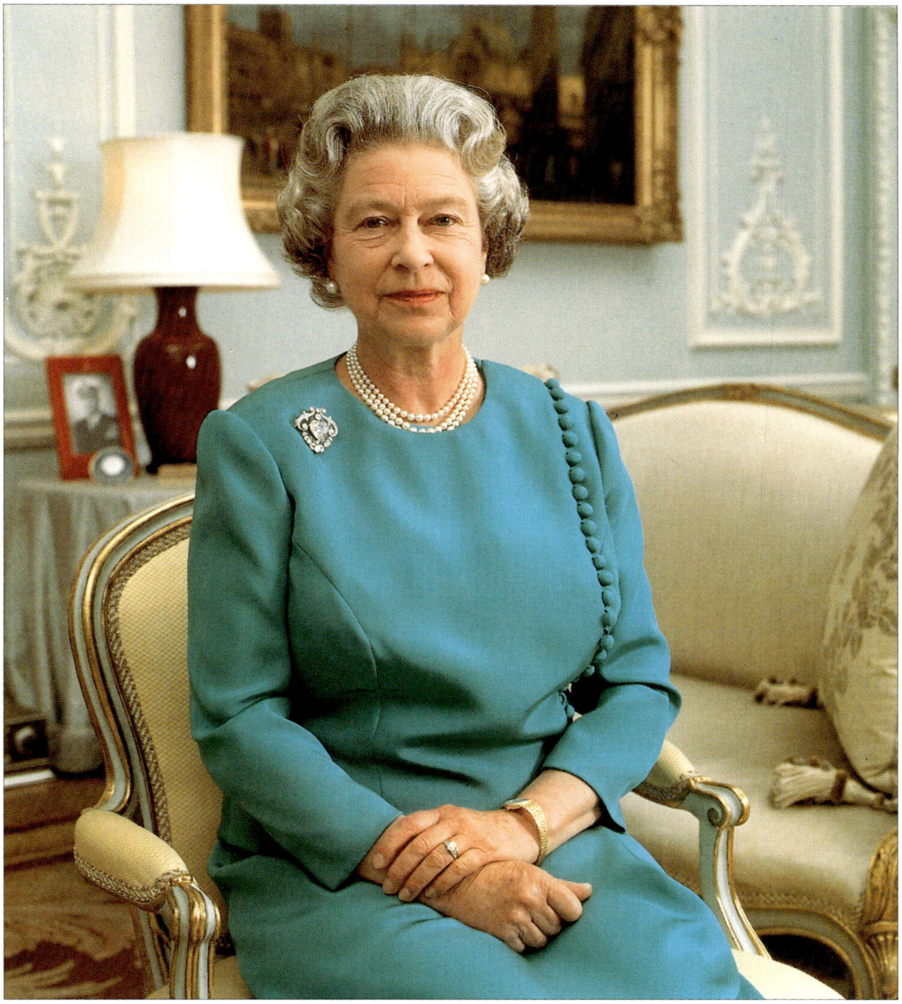

The Queen in 1991
This photograph by David Secombe, Sir Harry Secombe's son, was given to the Royal Anniversary Trust by Buckingham Palace.

ACKNOWLEDGEMENTS

Exhibition Acknowledgements

Sovereign Executive Committee
Jocelyn Stevens (Chairman), John Julius Norwich (Curator), Professor Christopher Frayling (College Curator), Ruth Anders (Project Director), Gerald Margolis (Finance Director), Professor Theo Crosby, Pedro Guedes, John Thackara, Hilary Bracegirdle, Julia Hawkins.

Special thanks to BBC Television, British Pathe News and Independent Television News. Additional archive footage supplied by British Movietone News and Central Office of Information.

Design by Pentagram. Research and procurement by Design Analysis International. Videowall by IE. Archive film research by Illuminations. Exhibition contractors – Button Eventures.

Picture Acknowledgements

Reproduced by gracious permission of Her Majesty the Queen: A State Banquet 1 and 2, The Queen's Dogs (RH page middle). Royal Collection, St James's Palace © 1992 Her Majesty the Queen: Coronation 1 (RH page below), The Coronation Dress (LH page above, RH page left), the Royal Collection 1 and 2, Royal Collectors, The Fabergé Collection, Windsor (RH page), Sandringham (RH page below), The Queen's Horses (LH page below). Windsor Castle, Royal Library © 1992 Her Majesty the Queen: Windsor (LH page below).

Specially commissioned photography by Geoff Dann: The Coronation Dress (RH page right), A State Banquet 1 and 2, Dressing To Be Seen 1 and 2, Memorabilia 1 and 2.

Camera Press: Front cover, Introduction, Princess Elizabeth (1931, 1935, 1938, 1941, 1942, 1944, 1945, 1948), The Coronation 2 (RH page). The Estate Office, Sandringham; Sandringham, (LH page, RH page above), The Queen's Horses (RH page above). Tim Graham: The Queen's Horses (LH page above). Glenn Harvey: The Queen's Horses (RH page below). Hulton Picture company: Princess Elizabeth (1951). Anwar Hussein: The Queen's Dogs (RH page below). Mirror Pictures: Princess Elizabeth (1950). Museum of London: Coronation 1 (coach). The National Postal Museum: Title page. Popperfoto: Princess Elizabeth (1926, 1927, 1928, 1929, 1930, 1932, 1934, 1936, 1939, 1940, 1946, 1947), Coronation 1 (RH page above). Press Association: Princess Elizabeth (1933, 1937). Reproduced by courtesy of Sir Hardy Amies: Dressing To Be Seen 1. Reproduced by courtesy of Susan Crawford: The Queen's Dogs (LH page). Reproduced by courtesy of Morris Green: The Coronation Dress (LH page below), Dressing To Be Seen 2 (LH page middle). Reproduced by courtesy of Hope and Glory Ltd: Royal Memorabilia 1 and 2. Reproduced by courtesy of Elizabeth Johnston: The Queen's Dogs (RH page above). Reproduced by courtesy of Captain George Mitcherson: The Coronation Dress (RH page right), Dressing To Be Seen 2 (LH page below right and RH page). Reproduced by courtesy of Hugo Vickers: Coronation 2 (LH page). Reproduced by permission of the Controller of Her Majesty's Stationery Office: Coronation 3. © The Royal Anniversary Trust: A Continuing Purpose. Syndication International: Princess Elizabeth (1943, 1949).

First published in Great Britain in 1992
by Collins & Brown Limited

ISBN 1 85585 123 7